The Mas

For my Ma Elizabeth, my wife Sarah
and my three daughters Alexandra, Charlotte and Louisa

This book is dedicated to all of the young chefs that I have worked with during my career – you have helped keep me young

The Masons Arms

Foreword

It is a privilege to write the foreword to Mark Dodson's long-awaited debut book. Mark is not only my great friend and an exceptional chef but an inspiration on so many levels. Like the man himself, his first book does not disappoint.

Having begun as sous chef at The Waterside Inn, Mark became head chef in 1988 and remains our longest-serving and only British cook to hold the position. Remarkably, he held three Michelin stars throughout his time at the pass, with and without me.

Before reflecting on Mark's qualities as a cook, I'd like to talk about the man himself. Mark is simply the most loyal and reliable person who has ever worked for me and has never let me down. It was not just at The Waterside Inn that Mark was my right-hand man, but he has since collaborated alongside me on many culinary projects worldwide.

Whenever I seek his assistance his response has always been the same: 'Yes chef'. In fact, I look upon Mark as I look upon my son. He is an honourable, thoughtful gentleman who instinctively and unconsciously does the right thing.

A hard-working and gifted chef, during the many years we have known one another not a bad word has passed between us, which is quite exceptional.

His consistency is another hallmark and during 18 years at The Waterside Inn, Mark did not miss a single day through sickness, which is incredible.

Heading a three Michelin star restaurant involves long, hard hours and wreaks an intense physical and emotional toll, which makes this record all the more extraordinary.

After leaving The Waterside Inn, Mark achieved a Michelin star in 2006 at The Masons Arms. He has retained it ever since, further exemplifying his hallmark consistency and skill.

When Mark decided to leave The Waterside Inn, he gave me plenty of warning yet, despite our readiness, we missed him. On the first day that he was not there, there was just a big hole. I found myself constantly searching for Mark, it took me time to adjust and accept he had gone.

Whilst Mark's name appears on the cover of this book, it is true to say his life and achievement as a chef is underpinned by his relationship to Sarah, his wife.

You know, I don't like the saying that 'behind every great man is a great woman', I prefer to say things differently. And in the case of Sarah, I would say she is a great supporter of Mark and so was also a great supporter of mine. I never heard her complain about the long hours that Mark worked.

Sarah is first, foremost and forever a fantastic wife and mother but is no less gifted as an exceptional businesswoman and restaurant manager, allowing Mark to concentrate on his craft as a chef. They have achieved a great balance in life with a shared life passion and business that defines them alongside a lovely family.

Together, Mark and Sarah are a strong team and demonstrate that beautiful things can come of such hard work and strength.

This Is Mine... features many favourite recipes enjoyed at The Masons Arms, which is delightful. I have eaten there a few times and the cooking is classic modern but with a little free interpretation, which I love. He has created unfussy food that people like to eat with no pretentions but a little twist here and there. Mark is a true chef and popular with team and clients alike.

In life and work, Mark sets high standards and invariably meets them. This book is another layer of achievement, the proof of my words alive on every page.

Mark does not want to grab the glory and score the goal: he just wants to cook and make people happy.

I am so delighted This Is Mine... is now in print so the whole world can meet and be inspired by this lovely man and enjoy his food. A good friend, a magnificent and unpretentious chef - I wish Mark every success with This Is Mine...

Michel Roux, OBE,
Global Ambassador
The Waterside Inn,
Three Michelin Stars

Contents

This is... Mark

Ma & Pa

I was never the boy who tugged at my Mum's apron strings to help cook, but I have always enjoyed food, both the eating and the artistry of it. My Mum is a good housewife cook, a term that she once took offence at, but in which she now finds my honest compliment.

Saturday was baking day: biscuits, choux pastry and various combinations of chocolate, Golden Syrup and Corn Flakes or Rice Krispies.

My Grandpa cooked his own piccalilli and chutneys. He also pickled his own onions in a stone jar and was equally at home plucking pheasants while sitting on a stool in the garage. So food, cooking and baking was a part of my life.

My Dad's only career advice to me was offered when I went to work at Le Talbooth in 1981. He advised me that as I was working in an establishment with an Egon Ronay Star, (it also had a Michelin Star but that was less high profile to him) I should stay at that level.

Little did any of us know that a year later I would be Sous-Chef there and in 1990, 19 years later, I would be the head chef of the Egon Ronay Restaurant of the Year.

Colchester

Record collecting was my thing when I was growing up in Colchester. It started in Budget Records, in Museum Street, where I'd buy ex-jukebox and 2nd hand records.

I moved to Howard Leach, in Church Walk, through the Prog and Glam eras, and then discovered Parrot Records, in Balkerne Passage, where I bought Punk and New Wave. I traced every band from The Beatles to Bowie and Bolan, via The Banshees and anyone else beginning with a B.

I was lucky enough to be in London in '78 & '79 and was going to gigs almost nightly, from small shows in pubs to bigger nights at The Marquee, The Electric Ballroom, The Music Machine, The Roundhouse, The Lyceum and The Hammersmith Odeon.

I've still got the list, and the ticket stubs.

Football

Giant killers! F.A. Cup 5th Round, 13th February 1971. Colchester United's Ray Crawford (second left) celebrates after scoring his second goal against the mighty Leeds United, to the delight of the Colchester United fans behind the goal, including a 13-year-old me (2nd along from the goal post), but to the dismay of (left-right) Gary Sprake, Jack Charlton, Paul Reaney and Paul Madeley of Leeds United.

Ship

Having left school without much in the way of qualifications I followed in the footsteps of my brother, who was in the Merchant Navy and was doing a summer on the North Sea Ferries. I ploughed my way across the North Sea on the Sealink Suffolk Ferry from Harwich to Zeebrugge, in Belgium, on an almost daily basis. Imagine my excitement at going to Hook of Holland a few times.

Having spent the best part of a year doing that and enjoying the atmosphere of the galley I decided to enrol at Colchester Institute to do my City and Guilds. I was then invited onto the 3rd year Diploma course, which at the time was pioneering as it was one of the first colleges to offer such a course. Thanks Malcolm.

The Waterside Inn

The Waterside Inn changed my life in many ways. We didn't count the hours there because we were one team, all striving for the same goal. We achieved it in 1985 with our 3rd Michelin Star.

I had gone there to eat and was lucky enough to have a chat with Michel Roux, who offered us a few desserts on the house. I wrote to thank him and asked about the possibility of a job.

There was a day's "stage" then a waiting list. However, six months later I was working there. I was 26 and signed up as a Commis with a 50% wage cut.

Sometimes you have to go down to go up.

It was also at The Waterside Inn that I met Sarah, without whom I would not be writing this, who became my wife.

We met at the village pub, which was called The Ringers. It was a Chef's hangout and it was a Sunday evening.

Bizarrely we were all talking French: thank you Mr Brown, those 2 years weren't a complete waste.

I think she liked my accent (Essex/French) and we met up again the following week.

Who would have thought that little pub would also achieve 3 Michelin Stars, albeit in a completely different guise as The Fat Duck.

I was privileged to work side by side and shoulder to shoulder with Michel Roux at The Waterside Inn.

I learnt so much there, I thought I would go there as "finishing school" but having spent my first 10 months on butchery, I decided I should stay a bit longer.

One evening as I was cleaning down my butchers block with the metal brush I was thrown 2 grapefruits to prepare into segments for a plain eater.

Having segmented the grapefruits I arranged the segments evenly on a plate and took it to the pass.

Within a couple of weeks I had changed sections so I must have done something right. In fact I stayed for 18 years and can honestly say there were very few days that I didn't enjoy or find challenging.

Career-wise, working at The Waterside would have been enough for me. It would already have been the pinnacle of my career, but to be asked to become Sous-Chef and then Head Chef was beyond my wildest dreams.

I still think of The Waterside every single day, we will be linked forever, it is such a special place and now when I go there it is like going home.

This is... Us

Mark and Sarah - By Mark

We met in 1984 in The Ringers, now the renowned Fat Duck, but back then it was the local pub for the Waterside Inn chefs.

It was a Sunday night, it must have been, or, perhaps a Monday.

Our fledgling relationship survived as Sarah was at college in Nottingham for three years, which coincided with me putting my head down and working my way up the ranks of the brigade to reach Head Chef in 1987.

We married in 1991 and there followed three beautiful, amazing daughters who have grown up in the most fantastic place, where there are less day-to-day pressures.

We arrived in Devon in June 2005 with an idea and a blackboard as a menu. Six months later we had a Michelin star.

Our aim was to create the sort of place that we would like to find if we were travelling or holidaying in the West Country. We wanted good honest food, featuring local ingredients wherever possible, that were presented with style and taste.

We opened on a small budget and have made a profit from day one.

Our working life has been harmonious, maybe because we both want the same thing. Despite the long hours and pressure we have never fallen out, however, sometimes a fairly large glass of wine is needed at the end of the evening.

Sarah and Mark - By Sarah

It was 1984. I met my friend in the pub, The Ringers, in Bray, and during the evening saw a good-looking chap waving at me and talking to me in French. He was from Essex, and that was it for me.

After college our romance survived my working week in London of Monday to Friday and Mark's of Tuesday to Sunday. At the Waterside they worked hard, a half day on a Sunday often meant starting at 8.30am and finishing at 5pm, but they were a family and Mark was so proud to be part of that family. I could see that, and was equally as proud to be part of it too.

Michel Roux is the most wonderful chef and friend to us and has been from the day I met him, as a tongue-tied 18-year-old. I know that he and his wife Robyn have the utmost respect for Mark - in fact I don't actually think Mark realises how much people do respect him and admire his talent.

When we moved to this tiny village I just knew how talented Mark was and that people would come. Mark has always been amazed at our success and whilst I never, ever take for granted what we have achieved here, I put it down to Mark's sheer drive, stamina (which astounds me), talent, experience and willingness to pass on his incredible knowledge to the younger chefs coming through. He learned from the best and, in my eyes, is the best.

Mark is my husband and best friend, he makes us complete - our unit of five plus our lovely Lab Tom, and I feel so proud to say…. He is Mine.

17

These are... 10 things about Mark

- Tottenham supporter

- Plays his music LOUD – and has a stunning collection of vinyl. Also keeps ticket stubs from gigs

- Makes the dog watch Match of the Day with him

- Loves cricket

- Makes the best Club Sandwich in the world, as well as the best Scrambled Eggs

- Ridicules his wife's music choices (which is fair - Mark has impeccable taste in music..., but don't tell Sarah that)

- Loves Quentin Tarantino films

- Loves walking the dog around Baggy Point and around the headland from Daymer Bay to Polzeath

- Would drink Burgundian wine when given the choice and a fine Armagnac or gin and tonic

- Holidays - family man..... Just the five of us

These are... basic principles

Before turning to the recipes, it will help you to have a basic working knowledge of how to use the book. These tips, therefore, should help make cooking that little bit easier – and the dishes much tastier.

Before starting to cook, assemble all of the ingredients and weigh them out. This may seem time consuming but will save you time in the end.

If you are cooking a recipe for 6 or 8 make sure you have enough space to lay out that number of plates. It sounds simple but balancing a warm plate on the toaster is not an option.

Cooking for relaxation shouldn't become stressful, so switch off your phone, be organised and have fun with it.

Very few things give the pleasure of presenting your family or friends with a wonderful meal, lovingly prepared.

I'm not a big fan of seasoning with pepper, I was taught that salt enhances flavour but pepper changes flavour. I find this to be true: pepper tends to sit on top of the flavour.

At the table I don't mind if someone seasons their food with pepper, provided that they have tasted it first. There are very few rules in cooking nowadays but one golden rule is to keep it seasonal.

The food of the season generally matches our appetites for that time of year, and don't be afraid to keep it simple.

As a chef the first thing I do when browsing a cookery book is say to myself " I wouldn't have done that" or "that would go well with ..." I'm not offended by that: cooking should be creative and we all have different ideas of what is appetising or not, and what goes well with what.

Stay within the framework but by all means change the odd garnish or sauce. Honestly I won't mind.

Unless specified

All butter used is unsalted.

All eggs are free range medium sized.

All flour used is T55 (a good all-round plain flour).

All sugar is caster sugar.

Olive oil when not specified is a light oil such as pomace olive oil.

Some of the pastry recipes call for sugar to be cooked to soft ball, which with the aid of a sugar thermometer is sugar cooked with a drop of water to 116°c.

19

This is ...

SOUPS

Chilled Melon, Ginger & Basil Soup

Ingredients for the ginger syrup

150g	water
150g	sugar
25g	root ginger, peeled and diced

Boil together and leave to infuse for 24 hours in the fridge.

Soup ingredients

2 x	honeydew melon, 750g each
2 x	charantais melon, 550g each
8 x	leaves of basil

Serves 6

This is perfect for a summer's evening. It is a light, refreshing soup that packs a gingery punch.

Skin, de-seed and cut the honeydew melon into pieces.

Skin and then halve the charantais melon. Remove the seeds and then using a melon baller scoop out rounds from the flesh. Cut the remainder into cubes and add to the other melon pieces. Blend together all of the melon with the syrup and basil leaves.

Pass through a fine chinois and add the melon balls, keep in the fridge until needed.

Serve nicely chilled in a soup bowl with the melon balls in the middle of the bowl and garnish with a leaf of basil or mint.

Gaspacho with Cucumber Sorbet

Ingredients

Gaspacho

500ml	tomato juice
100g	ripe plum tomatoes, cored and roughly chopped
20g	onion, chopped into dice
10g	peeled and crushed garlic
1	red pepper, cored, de-seeded and chopped
50g	cucumber, peeled and chopped
60ml	olive oil
15ml	red wine vinegar
1	slice of white bread, cubed with the crust removed first
	salt, pepper and tabasco sauce

Cucumber sorbet

1	cucumber
100ml	water
100g	sugar
20g	glucose
	juice of ½ a lemon.

Serves 4

This Andalusian classic is traditionally made and served with diced vegetables.

I prefer this more refined blended version, as does the younger Spanish generation. It is perfect for a summer's day.

In a suitable container, marinate all of the ingredients together for at least 12 hours.

Next, blend them all together in a liquidizer.

Pass the gaspacho through a fine sieve into a clean container and season with salt, pepper and a couple of drops of tabasco sauce.

Refrigerate until needed.

For the cucumber sorbet, peel and de-seed a cucumber, chop it roughly and then blend it in a food processor.

Boil together the water, sugar and glucose, adding the lemon juice.

Once the syrup is cold add the two parts together, pass through a sieve and churn. Keep the sorbet in the freezer until needed.

Serving:

At the time of serving ladle the gaspacho into chilled bowls with a ball of the cucumber sorbet in the centre.

Chef's note:

This can be served with diced peppers and deliciously crisp croutons if you prefer an alternative to cucumber sorbet.

Carrot, Orange, Ginger & Coriander Soup

Ingredients

450g	carrot
1	medium onion
1	stick of celery
1	clove of garlic
25g	fresh ginger
1	orange, peel and juice
600ml	vegetable stock or water
5g	fresh coriander leaves
15ml	olive oil
	salt and pepper

Serves 4

This silky smooth soup is delicious served either hot or chilled. If you do take the cold option try it with a spoon of natural yoghurt in the centre.

Peel and cut the fresh ginger into small dice, cut the carrot, onion and celery also into dice and peel and crush the garlic.

With a peeler remove the orange peel in wide strips and then halve and juice the orange.

Sweat the ginger, carrot, onion, garlic and celery in the olive oil in a suitable pan.

Once cooked a little without colour, add the stock, the orange juice and peel.

Simmer for around 40 minutes until the carrots are soft, skimming from time to time. Remove from the heat and finally add the coriander.

Remove the orange peel and then blend the soup in a liquidizer.

Once smooth pass it through a fine conical strainer to remove any last pieces of vegetables or fibres from the ginger.

Season to taste. Ideally there should be around 750ml of soup.

Re-boil the soup when needed. If there is coriander left over, a little can be chopped and added to some cream and a swirl can be added to each bowl at the last minute.

Chef's note:

The fresh ginger can be substituted with ground ginger but be aware that powdered spices will lose their strength over time once opened.

Roasted Tomato & Garlic Soup with Croûtons

Ingredients

12	overripe tomatoes, cores removed and roughly chopped
125g	onions, diced
125g	carrot, diced
60g	garlic, peeled and crushed
2	sticks of thyme
50g	soft dark brown sugar
30g	tomato purée
50ml	white wine
750ml	tomato juice
250ml	vegetable stock or water
	olive oil
	salt
	freshly ground pepper, 10 turns of the peppermill!
2	slices of white bread cut into cubes

Serves 6

A wonderfully warming, rich and hearty soup that is great in the Autumn or Winter, my family absolutely love it.

Why not double the recipe as any leftover will taste even better the next day?

In a large pan sweat off the onion, garlic and carrot with the olive oil, add to this the tomato purée.

In a separate frying pan, cook in three batches the tomatoes in olive oil with some salt and the sugar, add these to a large saucepan.

Finally, de-glaze with a little white wine and also pour this into the saucepan.

Add the tomato juice and cook out gently until the carrot is soft.

As the soup thickens during cooking add the vegetable stock to keep a good consistency.

Once cooked, blend and pass the soup through a fine sieve.

Season with salt and the freshly ground pepper.

Cut the crusts off the white bread and cut it into cubes and then pan fry gently in oil until golden, for extra richness add a knob of butter ⅔ of the way through cooking.

Drain on a sheet of absorbent paper before serving.

Garnish with chilli oil and some croûtons served separately.

Shellfish Bisque with Sole Raviolo

Ingredients

750g	lobster or crab shells
	olive oil
1	medium onion, 75g
2	carrots, 125g
2	cloves of garlic
1	fennel bulb, 100g
1	stick of celery
4	sticks of thyme
50g	tomato purée
50ml	brandy
125ml	white wine
1.5l	fish stock
400ml	double cream

Garnish

1	carrot
1	courgette

Mousse filling

150g	lemon sole fillet
1	egg white
200ml	double cream
1	pinch cayenne
	salt
	chives

Pasta

125g	00 pasta flour
1	egg yolk
1	whole egg
1	tsp olive oil
1	pinch of salt

Serves 6

Cut the vegetables into a large dice and crush the garlic. Cover the bottom of a suitable pan with olive oil and when nice and hot add the vegetables and cook with a little colour before adding the tomato purée. Cook for a further 5 minutes and then flame with the brandy.

A minute later add half of the white wine and cook for 2 minutes. In a separate pan cook off the shells in a little hot oil. Once cooking nicely, drain off the oil and deglaze with the remaining wine. Add the shells to the vegetables and cover with fish stock, bring to the boil, skim and leave to cook gently for 1½ hours.

Once cooked pass the liquid through a fine strainer and cook to reduce to 450ml. Pass again and leave to cool.

Refrigerated, this bisque base will keep for 2-3 days.

For the mousse filling, dice the sole fillet and blend to a paste in a food processor with the egg white and a pinch of salt. Rub it through a drum sieve. Place the paste in a bowl on ice and gradually beat in the double cream in about 20ml measures.

Once incorporated add some snipped chives, season and reserve.

To make the raviolo pasta, combine the flour, salt and eggs in a food processor and then add the oil, drop by drop, to form a crumbly texture.

Form the dough by hand into a flat rectangular shape, cling film and refrigerate to rest for 2 hours.

Roll out the pasta by putting it through a pasta roller, decreasing the thickness each time and finishing when it is as thin as possible.

Cut the pasta in half so that you have two sheets of about 50cm in length.

Lay the first sheet of pasta onto a work surface dusted with flour and spoon the mousse evenly into 6 piles leaving a good gap in between each one.

Cover the mousse with the remaining pasta. Push down the mousse with the reverse of a 4cm cutter to remove any air.

Cut out the raviolo with a 6cm cutter. Place them onto a floured tray and refrigerate until needed.

Serving:

At the time of serving re-heat the bisque, 75ml per person, and add 75ml double cream. Re-boil gently for a couple of minutes and season.

Poach the ravioli for 5 minutes, place into soup bowls, pour on the bisque and garnish with some small carrot and courgette balls.

Chef's note:

The mousse and pasta recipe will give you more than you need but these ravioli will freeze well and can be cooked from frozen.

If just serving as a bisque without the ravioli, allow 50% more per person, in which case this recipe will give 4 good portions.

This is ...

STARTERS

Smoked Chicken with Thai Style Salad

Salad ingredients

1	head Chinese leaves, finely shredded
1	bunch spring onion, cut into thin circles
1	piecered chilli, seeds removed and finely diced
5g	coriander leaves, chopped
60g	toasted flaked almonds
40g	salted peanuts

Dressing

60ml	rice wine vinegar
60ml	vegetable oil
50ml	light soy sauce
50ml	fish sauce
60g	caster sugar

Smoked chicken

allow 1 breast per two portions

Serves 4

This is such a favourite from my Waterside days. I could (almost) eat this every day. It's a great starter or light main course served with a beautifully crisp white wine.

To make the dressing, mix together all of the ingredients and warm them in a suitable pan to dissolve the sugar.

Once the sugar has dissolved, remove the mix from the heat and transfer it to a bowl and then mix in all the salad ingredients. Leave in the fridge to infuse.

This wonderfully fragrant salad can easily be made the day before needed.

Leaving the skin and the under-fillet on, salt the breasts for 20 minutes before rinsing and patting dry.

Fill the bottom of the smoker with Oak chippings and heat the smoker. When it is going well lightly oil the chicken and lay it onto the grill rack part of the smoker.

Cover it with the lid and reduce the heat to a give a gentle smoke. Leave to smoke for 15-20 minutes.

A good way of checking that the chicken is cooked is to lift the under-fillet to look at the breast which should now be white. If you're not sure carefully make a small cut at the thickest part of the breast to double check. It's better to be safe than sorry!

Leave the chicken to cool before slicing. I prefer the chicken served at an ambient temperature but the chicken once refrigerated will be perfect the next day.

When it comes to serving, slice the chicken neatly onto the salad and garnish with salad leaves, salted peanuts and herbs

Chef's note:

If no smoker is available it's fine to buy a smoked chicken breast.

Try to find one that is not too dark and smoky.

Black Treacle-Cured Salmon

Ingredients

1	side of salmon weighing approximately 1.2kg

Cure

400g	sea salt
600g	caster sugar
15g	ground black pepper
500ml	orange juice
1 tsp	caraway seeds
1	lemon juice and zest
1 tbsp	black treacle, warmed through to help it mix

Lemon vinaigrette

100ml	white wine vinegar
50g	caster sugar
300ml	olive oil
2	dessert spoons of Dijon mustard
2	lemon zest, finely grated and juice

Cumin cream (x4)

100ml	double cream
2	good pinches of ground cumin
	salt

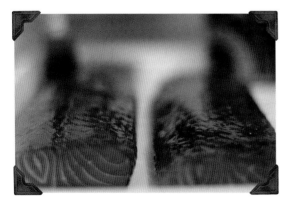

Serves 12

Mix together all the ingredients for the cure only using half the black treacle.

Leave the skin on the salmon and score it 4 or 5 times, place in the cure and cover with cling film.

The salmon will take 48 hours to cure and will need to be turned after 24 hours.

Once ready, wash off the cure and pat dry.

Brush again with the remaining warmed black treacle.

Wrap in cling film and refrigerate.

Cut thinly as required and serve either in slices or rolled.

To make the lemon vinaigrette, gently heat the sugar in the vinegar and, once dissolved, leave to cool.

Use a hand blender to mix in the mustard, lemon juice and zest.

Finally, slowly blend in the oil and reserve until needed.

For the cumin cream, simply whisk together the cream and the cumin in a bowl until the cream will stand up.

Season and refrigerate.

Chef's note:

A simple garnish to accompany this salmon is neatly cut cubes of cucumber and beetroot with dill, caviar and salmon caviar and a quenelle of the cumin cream.

Salad of Crab with Citrus & Star Anise

Ingredients

Crab

1	cock crab, approximately 1.2kg giving 240g white crab meat
150g	crème fraiche or mayonnaise
8	leaves coriander, finely chopped
1	orange
	salt & freshly ground pepper

Cucumber

1	cucumber
100g	white wine vinegar
50g	sugar

Dressing

3	star anise
200ml	orange juice
2	pinches of sugar
1	teaspoon of white wine vinegar
100ml	good quality olive oil
1	pinch of salt

Garnish

2	oranges or pink grapefruit

Serves 4

If you are not too squeamish it is always preferable to cook your own crab. Remember when buying a live crab, it should be just that.

If not, buy good quality hand-picked white crab meat, which will be an excellent substitute.

Cucumber

Boil together the white wine vinegar and sugar. Cut the cucumber into long "spaghetti" strips, avoiding the seeds in the centre. While boiling, add the cucumber and then remove from the heat immediately. Leave the cucumber to cool in the liquid.

This cucumber will keep for at least 24 hours refrigerated, so can be made in advance.

Dressing

Boil together the orange juice, sugar and star anise. Reduce by half, leaving 100ml of liquid.

Leave to cool and infuse for at least 3 hours. Add the white wine vinegar and the salt and then with the aid of a hand blender incorporate the olive oil.

Once again this can be made in advance and will keep at least 24 hours refrigerated.

Serving:

Segment the citrus fruit for garnish.

In a bowl combine the crab meat, crème fraiche or mayonnaise and coriander. Season with a little salt and some freshly ground pepper.

Drain and neatly arrange some of the cucumber on the plates and on top of this carefully place the crab mixture.

Garnish with the fruit segments and some salad leaves, serve immediately.

Delicious.

Seared Peppered Tuna with Oriental Salad

Ingredients

600g	tuna
15ml	red wine vinegar
100ml	soy sauce
100ml	sesame oil
90g	sugar
1	head chinese leaf salad
1	chopped red chilli
3	bunches of spring onions
2	cloves of garlic
25g	root ginger
1	lime
5g	chopped fresh coriander leaves
5g	toasted sesame seeds

Sesame biscuit (optional)

30g	sesame seeds
15g	poppy seeds
30g	icing sugar
20g	flour
10ml	orange juice
35g	melted unsalted butter
1	pinch of salt

Serves 6

I love this recipe. It has been with me since the 2000s I think. It started at The Waterside and then we did the same salad at Cliveden with Langoustine Beignets. Now that is luxury!

In a suitable pan bring to the boil the red wine vinegar, soy sauce, sesame oil and sugar.

Then add the head of chinese leaf salad, shredded with the majority of the white stem removed, chopped red chilli, I prefer the seeds removed, spring onions, trimmed and cut into circles, cloves of garlic, peeled and crushed into a paste.

Add the root ginger, peeled and finely grated lime with the zest finely grated and the juice juiced, chopped fresh coriander leaves and toasted sesame seeds.

Cut the tuna fillet into 1 inch width batons of about 100g per portion. Wrap them in oiled cling film and season with salt and coarsely ground black and white peppercorns. Roll them tightly, tie off the ends and then poach them in simmering water for a minute, once the outside starts to go brown remove them.

Cut open the cling film and remove the tuna, then roll the batons in hot oil to colour the outside. Slice and serve on the salad.

For the (optional) sesame biscuit combine all of the ingredients and leave it to set in the fridge for a couple of hours before spreading thinly on a baking sheet. Bake in a pre-heated oven at 180°c for approximately 4 minutes, until golden.

Chefs note:

The salad once prepared can easily be kept for 24 hours, it gets better! Also the tuna can easily be rolled into the cling film the day before cooking them, mis-en-place!

Soy, Mirin & Yuzu Marinated Salmon, Salad of White Radish, Apple & Cucumber

Ingredients

Salmon

400g	salmon fillet, skinned and trimmed
100ml	soy sauce
50ml	yuzu juice
50ml	mirin
½	lemon, juiced
1	teaspoon of coriander seeds, toasted and crushed

Salad

75ml	white wine vinegar
75g	caster sugar
½	mooli, thinly sliced
4	radishes, thinly sliced
1	granny smith apple, skin on, thinly sliced
½	cucumber, skin on thinly sliced

Garnish

1	cube of fresh horseradish
15g	vermicelli rice noodles
	micro herbs

Serves 4

For the salad pickling liquor, add the vinegar and sugar to a pan and bring to the boil with a pinch of salt.

Stir until the sugar is completely dissolved, then remove from the heat.

Add the sliced mooli, radish, apple and cucumber and set aside to lightly pickle for 1-2 hours.

To prepare the salmon, mix all of the marinade ingredients together in a large container and thinly slice the salmon.

2 minutes before you are ready to serve, submerge the salmon slices in the marinade for a maximum of 2 minutes - any longer and it will begin to "cook" the fish.

Lightly separate the noodles and deep-fry in small batches at 180°c until puffed up and crispy - this should take around 20-30 seconds.

Remove, season and drain on an absorbent towel.

To serve, arrange the slices of the marinated salmon onto each plate.

Place the salad neatly in the middle and garnish with some micro herbs.

Finally grate over some fresh horseradish and top the dish off with the crispy rice noodles at the last moment.

Chicken and Ham Hock Terrine with Leeks

Ingredients

1	ham hock, 1.5kg
2	chickens, 1.25kg each
1	leek, 250g finely sliced
100ml	white wine
1	shallot, sliced
1	lemon quartered
75g	butter
1	bay leaf
1	medium sized onion, halved through the core
1	stick of celery, cut in two
1	carrot, peeled and halved lengthways
6	parsley stalks
3	leaves gelatine
	salt, pepper and a pinch of white peppercorns

Serves 16

Soak the ham hock overnight and the following day give it a good rinse in cold water. Transfer it into a suitable saucepan. Cover with water and add the bay leaf, onion, celery, carrot, peppercorns and parsley stalks. Bring to the boil and leave to simmer. It will take up to 3 hours to cook.

A good way of testing to see if it is cooked is to pull out the small bone beside the knuckle which will only come out once cooked. Leave to cool in the cooking liquor.

Once the ham hock has been on for about 1½ hours, season, lightly oil and roast the two chickens in a suitable roasting tray surrounded by the lemon, shallot and white wine. The chicken should be cooked thoroughly so allow 1½ hours at 170°c. Don't let the roasting tray go dry as the cooking liquor is needed later, if necessary add a little water.

In a separate pan sauté the leeks in the butter, cooked but still retaining a crunch.

The chickens and ham hock should be ready at around the same time. Once manageable, remove the skin and as much fat as possible from the ham hock. Shred the meat between your fingers into a bowl.

Pass the cooking juice from the chicken roasting tray into a measuring jug and remove any fat. If necessary top up with some of the ham liquor to give 200ml.

Soak the gelatine in cold water and add to the liquor, which may need to be warmed to dissolve the gelatine.

Carefully remove the skin from the chicken breasts in one large piece if you can, as that can be dried out in a low oven and then used to crumble onto the top of the terrine when serving.

Now shred the meat from the chickens through your fingers, being careful not to get any small pieces of bone in with the meat.
Mix together the ham and the chicken.

Add the leeks and then pass the liquor onto that. Season and then set in a tray 30cm x 22cm and 3cm deep, which has been lined with cling film with an overlap. Once filled fold over the overlap, sealing the terrine.

Press the terrine with some weight and leave overnight in the fridge before serving.

Chef's note:

Traditionally the bone removed from the ham hock was used to serve mustard with the poached ham. A drop of Dijon mustard would be great with this terrine. Try it with our pea and mint vinaigrette.

Duck Liver Parfait, Rhubarb Chutney

Ingredients

Duck liver parfait

625g	duck livers, de-nerved
625g	clarified unsalted butter, warm
6	whole eggs
100ml	port
100g	redcurrant jelly
3	good pinches of salt

Rhubarb chutney

1kg	rhubarb
500g	sultanas
1kg	soft dark brown sugar
25g	lemons into juice
25g	garlic, crushed
25g	salt
25g	fresh ginger, grated or cut into small dice
500ml	white wine vinegar

Serves 16

Follow this recipe and you'll make sure you have no more grey and grainy chicken or duck liver parfaits ever again.
Butter the terrine well with soft but not melted butter and refrigerate, allow 25g of butter for this.

In a pan cook together the port and redcurrant jelly until it thickens.

Place the duck livers in a food processor and blend, add the eggs, the warm clarified butter, the port mixture and season with the salt.

Pass the mixture through a fine sieve to remove any fibres and pour it into the terrine. Wipe the edges and cover it with cling film for the baking process.

Cook in a bain-marie in a pre-heated oven at 140°c for approximately 1 hour 10 minutes. A needle inserted into the middle of the terrine should come out clean when it is cooked. Remember the terrine will carry on cooking for a bit once out of the oven and it should be pink in colour when serving.

Leave the terrine to cool before refrigerating for at least 12 hours before serving. To de-mould the terrine when needed, stand it in a little warm water and heat the blade of a small palette knife.

Run it around the edge of the terrine and turn it out with a "bang" directly onto a board.

The recipe for rhubarb chutney has been passed down by my great grandmother on my mother's side, it originates in the 19th century and I am the 4th generation to make it, I love tradition...and I love this chutney! In a thick bottom pan, cook until sticky!

Chefs note:

Clarified butter is made by gently melting unsalted butter over water. Once melted, skim the top and pass the butter leaving behind the milky residue which is not needed.

The duck livers can easily be replaced by chicken livers, I just feel the duck livers add a bit more richness.

The same recipe can be used for individual portions. Just be careful of the cooking time!

Seared Scallops with Pear & Vanilla

Ingredients

12	large scallops
3	pears
150ml	red wine
150g	sugar
50g	soft cream cheese
½	lime, juice and zest
1	finely chopped shallot
25ml	Noilly Prat or other dry vermouth
50ml	fish stock
60ml	double cream
¼	vanilla pod, split and with the seeds scraped with a knife micro cress, chervil or salad garnish

Serves 6

We always have scallops somewhere on the menu – they are delicate but full of flavour and so popular.

Peel and slice the pears with a mandolin to get 12 good long slices and with the smaller slices cut out 12 x 3cm discs. With the same 3cm cutter remove any seeds and core from the long slices.

Any trimmings of pear could be cooked with a little sugar and water until soft and then puréed smooth.

Bring the red wine and sugar to the boil and then add the pear slices and discs. Bring back to the boil and, depending on the ripeness of the pears, cook for a minute or two.

Once cooked if left for up to 24 hours the pears will take on a lovely burgundy colour.

For the sauce, in a pan cook together the chopped shallot and vermouth. When almost dry, add the fish stock and reduce again, then add the double cream and vanilla. Bring to the boil and leave to simmer gently until the sauce is of a good consistency. Pass through a fine sieve and season.

Zest and juice the ½ lime and mix well into the cream cheese to make the lime cream.

Serving:

Place three slices of pear onto each plate and in the centre of each pear put a touch of the lime cream. Sear the scallops in a smoking hot pan. When the scallop is hot to the touch and nicely coloured it will be cooked.

Place a scallop in the centre of each pear and then add a little of the pear purée, if using, to each plate. Gently pour on a little of the vermouth sauce. Top each of the scallops with a pear disc, and garnish with a little salad and herbs.

Chef's note:

Care should be taken when cooking the scallops. If unsure it is better to check the degree of cooking, so with the aid of a small knife make a small cut into one of the scallops to check the inside, the scallops can always be returned to the pan and cooked more if needed.

Puff Pastry of Mushroom Duxelles with St Enodoc Asparagus, Poached Egg & Hollandaise Sauce

Ingredients for cases

160g   puff pastry

Duxelles

500g   button mushrooms finely chopped by hand
4   finely chopped shallots
200ml   double cream
olive oil

Poached eggs

4   eggs
splash of white wine vinegar

Hollandaise sauce

4   10g tarragon
20g   chopped shallots
5g   crushed white peppercorns
75ml   white wine vinegar
40ml   white wine
3   egg yolks
180g   clarified butter, unsalted

Asparagus

24   St Enodoc asparagus tips

Serves 4

I love this asparagus and the area it comes from. I was introduced to Daymer Bay by Sarah and her family in the 90s. It really is one of the most beautiful places. Nothing gives me more pleasure than to climb to the top of Brae Hill and look past the tiny St Enodoc church to see the field where this wonderful asparagus grows, seasoned by the salty coastal winds, for its all-too-short season.

To make pastry cases, roll out 160g of puff pastry into a square approximately 20cm x 20cm. From this cut out 4 circles of 8cm. Egg wash them and then make an indent in the centre with a 5cm cutter. Leave to rest and then bake them in the oven until risen and golden for approximately 12 mins at 180°c. Once cool cut around the marking, remove the lid and pull out some of the undercooked centre.

For the duxelles, sweat the shallot in a little oil, add the mushrooms and cook until almost dry. Finally add the cream and cook until it thickens. Season with a little salt and pepper.

Fill a deep saucepan with water and a splash of white wine vinegar. Bring to the boil and reduce the heat to the point where there are bubbles just forming on the bottom of the pan. Break the eggs onto 4 saucers and, one by one, add them gently into the water each time giving the water a stir in a circular motion. The eggs will be cooked soft after 3 minutes. Trim off any loose egg white so that the egg is a nice even shape. If they are not being used at once, drop them into cold water to be re-heated when serving.

To make the hollandaise sauce, for the reduction you will need the tarragon, chopped shallots, crushed white peppercorns, white wine vinegar and white wine.

Boil together all of the above and then simmer for a couple of minutes. Pass through a sieve before using. You may not need all of the reduction, but it will keep well in the fridge.

Whisk the yolks over heat with a touch of the reduction to ribbon stage. Gently add the warmed clarified butter drop by drop. As the sauce thickens let it down with more of the reduction, season with a pinch of salt.

Cooking and serving:

Peel the asparagus tips and cook them in a pan of boiling water with a pinch of salt. Once they are cooked brush them with a little melted butter.

Fill the pastry cases with the duxelles and top with the poached eggs. Cover generously with the hollandaise sauce and garnish with some snipped chives and chervil.

Chef's note:

To clarify the butter, cut it into cubes place in a suitable container and stand in a bain-marie on the stove until it melts and becomes clear. Skim any impurities from the top and decant the butter leaving behind the milky residue.

Breasts of Quail with Grapes, Walnuts & Sauternes Jus

Ingredients

6   quail

Sauternes jus

200g	quail legs or carcass
1	carrot, chopped
1	shallot, chopped
1	sprig of thyme
100ml	Sauternes
100ml	chicken stock
100ml	veal stock

Walnuts, grapes and spinach

12	walnut halves
12	ripe red grapes
200g	spinach

Serves 4

This simple dish relies on some skillful butchery to give a sharp presentation.

Remove the wishbones from the quail.

Take off the breasts and legs leaving only the last wing joint on the breast.

Chop off the tiny knuckle and clean away any meat from the bone with a sharp knife. Allow three breasts per portion.

In a little oil, colour the quail legs or carcasses gently with the shallot, carrot and thyme.

Pour off any excess oil and de-glaze with the Sauternes.

Once reduced, add the chicken and veal stocks. Leave to cook gently for a good 20 minutes, skimming from time to time.

Pass through a fine strainer and return to the heat to reduce slightly.

Next, blanch the walnut halves in milk and carefully peel off the outside skin. Peel, halve and de-seed the grapes. De-vein, wash and dry the spinach.

Cooking and serving:

Season and gently pan fry the quail breasts skin-side first, they will only take 2 minutes on each side.

Lift up the small fillet on the underside to check the cooking.

Sauté the spinach in a knob of butter drain and place in the centre of the plates. Drop the grapes and walnuts into the sauce to warm through.

Place the quail breasts around the spinach and finally pour the sauce around, dividing the grapes and walnuts equally.

Chef's note:

Just four ingredients all in harmony with each other, this formula will always give you a perfect dish.

56

Smoked Scallops with Wasabi, Noodles & Vermouth Sauce

Ingredients

12	scallops, retaining the two nicest corals
1	cucumber
240g	udon noodles
100g	carrot, cut into julienne
40g	mange-tout, cut into julienne
	soy sauce
	toasted sesame seeds

For the purée

2	medium parsnips, 225g
	100 ml double cream
	wasabi paste to taste

For the sauce

25ml	Noilly Prat, or other dry vermouth
1	chopped shallot
100ml	double cream
2	corals from the scallops

Serves 4

This dish proved so popular, and, wanting to smoke the scallops to order, we had many a chaotic service.

For the purée, peel the parsnips and cut them into 2cm dice, cover with water, add a pinch of salt and cook until soft. Drain well and return to the pan.

Stir them round to evaporate the last of the liquid. Add the double cream and cook a little further. Blend in a liquidizer, season to taste with a pea-sized drop of wasabi, reserve and keep hot.

To make the sauce, in a suitable pan reduce the Noilly Prat with the chopped shallot, then add the cream and thicken a little by reduction.

Pass the sauce onto the corals, liquidize and re-pass. Keep warm but once the coral has been added the sauce must not boil.

Make sure that the scallops are nicely cleaned: they can be lightly rinsed but don't leave them in water or they will lose their beautiful, subtle flavour.

In the smoker put some oak sawdust and cover the grill with tin foil. Lightly oil and season the scallops.

Once the smoker is going gently place the scallops onto the foil.

Cover with the lid and leave to smoke, depending on the size of the scallops and the heat of the smoker the scallops will be cooked in about 5 minutes. This can be checked by inserting a needle or the tip of a knife into the scallop which should be warm in the centre.

Re-heat the udon noodles in lightly salted boiling water with the julienne of carrot and the julienne of mange-tout.

Drain and then toss in a little soy sauce and dress on the plate.

Peel the cucumber and then cut and hollow 3 thick slices per portion, reheat in boiling water when required and place on top of the noodles. Fill with the parsnip and wasabi purée.

Place the scallops neatly on top of the cucumber rings and sprinkle with a few toasted sesame seeds.

Croquette of Ham Hock with Pea Purée, Mint Butter Sauce

Ingredients

Ham hock

1	good-sized ham hock

Croquettes

400g	flaked meat from the ham hock
400g	potato purée
1	egg yolk, but the mix may need more, depending on the dryness of the potato

Mint butter sauce

5g	fresh mint leaves, chopped
15g	peeled and chopped shallots
5g	crushed white peppercorns
70ml	white wine vinegar
35ml	white wine
50ml	double cream
160g	unsalted butter, cubed

Pea purée

200g	frozen peas
200ml	water
20ml	olive oil
1	pinch of salt
1	pinch of sugar
1	dash of double cream

Serves 8

This is a beautiful adaptation of the classic combination of ham, peas and mint.

Soak the ham hock overnight in plenty of water. The following, day rinse it off and place it into a suitable pan.

Cover it with water, add a bay leaf, a few white peppercorns, a carrot peeled and cut lengthways, an onion halved, some parsley stalks and a couple of celery sticks.

Bring it to the boil and then reduce the heat to a simmer. Cook for 3-4 hours until the meat is falling off the bone.

To form the croquettes use the flaked meat from the ham hock, potato purée and 1 egg yolk (the mix may need more egg yolk, depending on the dryness of the potato).

Set in a tray and refrigerate and once set portion into eight equal pieces.

For the mint butter sauce use a thick-bottom pan and boil together all of the ingredients with the exception of the butter and cream.

When almost dry, add the double cream and bring to the boil. Remove from the heat and gently stir or shake in the butter. At this point the sauce must not boil.

Pass the sauce through a fine sieve and finish it with some fine julienne of mint.

To make the pea purée boil together the water, oil, salt and sugar then add the peas and cook well (8 minutes). Drain the peas in the pan and add the dash of cream. Blend smoothly in a liquidizer using some of the cooking liquor to adjust the consistency to give a vibrant and smooth purée.

Serving:

Flour, egg wash and breadcrumb the croquettes and gently pan fry them, warm the pea purée and place in the centre of the plate.

Once cooked until golden, cut the croquettes in half and place on top. Pour some sauce around the outside of the dish and garnish with some pea shoots and julienne of raw carrot.

Smoked Haddock Risotto with Parmesan and a Poached Egg, Grain Mustard Sauce

Ingredients

200g	smoked haddock fillet, skinned and pin boned
150ml	double cream
175g	carnaroli risotto rice
100ml	white wine
50g	finely chopped onion
1tbsp	olive oil
600ml	fish stock
50g	finely grated parmesan cheese
4	eggs for poaching
1	splash of white wine vinegar

For the sauce

125ml	double cream
25g	grain mustard
	salt & pepper

Serves 4

This, quite simply, is the ultimate kedgeree.

Heat the oil in a pan, sweat the onions so they are soft but not coloured.

Add the rice to the pan and stir with a spatula until the rice is coated with the oil.

Add the white wine and bring it to the boil.

Don't stir the rice until the wine is boiling. Then slowly add the stock, ladle by ladle, and keep stirring often until each ladleful is absorbed.

Keep stirring the stock in until the rice is tender, but allowing for a slight resistance to the bite. This should take about 15-18 minutes. Remove the risotto from the heat.

In a separate pan, poach the haddock in 150ml double cream. Once cooked, flake the haddock and gently stir it into the rice with the cream along with the grated parmesan.

Keep the risotto warm while you poach the eggs.

To poach the eggs, bring a deep pan of water to the boil. Add a splash of vinegar to the water, before reducing to a gentle simmer.

Break the eggs into the pan. Stir the water in a circular motion to stop the egg staying on the bottom of the pan. Poach them for 3 minutes.

Lift each egg out with a slotted spoon and drain briefly on kitchen paper.

For the sauce, simply boil together the double cream and the grain mustard and season with salt and pepper. Reserve until required.

Serving:

Divide the risotto between four plates and top each serving with a poached egg, re-boil and a good spoon of sauce.

Garnish with some rocket leaves, chervil, sun dried tomatoes and parmesan shavings.

This is ...

MAINS

Arancini with Beetroot Three Ways

Ingredients

Arancini

½	onion, finely chopped
	olive oil, splash of
200g	carnaroli rice
50ml	white wine
375ml	vegetable stock
50g	Parmesan cheese, finely grated
75ml	double cream
90g	mozzarella cheese, 12 even cubes
	flour, egg, beaten with a pinch of salt and breadcrumbs, to pané

Horseradish cream

80ml	double cream
1 tsp	creamed horseradish

Turned beetroots

2	medium beetroots, peeled
25g	soft light brown sugar
50ml	red wine vinegar

Beetroot purée

300g	raw beetroot, peeled and roughly diced
200ml	double cream
	salt and pepper

Pickled beetroot

1	medium golden beetroot, enough for 12 good round slices
200ml	white wine vinegar
100g	sugar

Garnish

	salad leaves or cress
	horseradish, freshly grated

Serves 4

Arancini originate in Italy and there are a number of regional variations, which differ in fillings and size. They are stuffed balls of risotto that are frequently filled with cheese or ragu, then coated in bread crumbs and deep fried. The texture is delightful. This version combines soft, creamy cheese with the flavours of sweet, earthy beetroots. It's a match made in heaven.

Arancini

Sweat the onion in a pan with a little oil, without colouring, until soft. Add the rice and stir to coat the grains in oil. Pour the white wine into the pan and bring to the boil without stirring. Add the vegetable stock, drop by drop, until the rice is cooked but with a little 'bite' remaining. Add both the Parmesan and the cream before bringing back to boil. Season the mixture, then spread the risotto onto a tray. Refrigerate until cold.

Shape the rice around the cubes of mozzarella. Dust in the flour, egg wash and then the breadcrumbs. Deep fry at 170°c until golden. Drain and season.

Turned beetroots

Cut each beetroot into 12 equal segments. Shape the segments with the aid of a sharp knife, turning them into barrel shapes to remove the hard edges.
Put the 24 turned beetroot barrels into a pan and cook with the sugar and vinegar, stirring occasionally. As the beetroots cook, the liquor will evaporate leaving a glaze on them.

Beetroot purée

Cook the diced beetroot in lightly salted water on a low heat. Leave to cook until soft, this could take up to 2 hours and you may need to top up the water. When soft, drain well and return to the pan. Stir the beetroot around to evaporate the last of the liquid. Add the double cream, leave to cook and thicken. Once the mixture has thickened, place into a blender and blend until smooth. Season to taste, reserve and keep hot.

Pickled beetroot

Peel and finely slice the golden beetroot. Combine the sugar and vinegar in a pan and bring to the boil. Add the sliced beetroot, and then leave them to cool in the pickling syrup.

Make a swirl of purée on the plate. Dot around the horseradish cream. Place the arancini onto the plate with the 'turned' beetroots and the pickled beetroots (which can be rolled up). Garnish with some delicate salad leaves or cress. Finish with the freshly grated horseradish.

Chef's note:

A great way to use up leftover risotto, the Italian equivalent of bubble and squeak.

Potato Pancakes with Cèpe Mushrooms

Ingredients

1	large baking potato, giving 150g of pulp
10g	flour
25ml	double cream
2	eggs
	salt & pepper

Garnish

16	pieces of sundried tomatoes
50g	cèpe mushrooms
1	courgette cut in to ribbons

Duxelles

250g	button mushrooms
125g	cèpe mushrooms
2	shallots, 60g
100ml	double cream
	olive oil
	salt & pepper

Serves 4

I love making these pancakes. If you are like me, you will need to taste one early on... but only to make sure they are as good as they look and smell.

Score the potato around its middle with the tip of a sharp knife and then bake it until soft for about an hour at 180°c in a pre-heated oven. Once cooked leave it to cool so that it is manageable and then scoop out the inside of the potato and discard the skin.

Place the potato pulp into a tall container and add the flour, cream and eggs, blend with a stick blender and season with salt and pepper.

Brush a little oil in a non-stick pan and spoon in some of the mixture into a circular shape, turning them once, cook the pancakes gently on both sides. Continue until all of the mixture is used.

For the duxelles, chop the mushrooms finely with a large knife. Also finely chop the shallot and sweat it in a drop of olive oil.

Once cooked, but without colour, add the mushrooms to the pan. Cook again until almost dry before adding the cream. Bring back to the boil and cook a little to thicken, season and set to one side.

Serving:

Gently re-heat the pancakes and sandwich the duxelles in between two of them per portion.

Garnish with some grilled courgettes, sun dried tomatoes and some sauteéd cèpe mushrooms cooked together with a little chopped shallot and chopped parsley. Around the edge of the plate drizzle a little chilli oil and balsamic vinegar.

Chef's note:

As tempting as it may be to take a short cut, it's much better to hand chop the mushrooms for the duxelles rather than using a food processor where they may become mushy.

The pancakes will freeze beautifully well between squares of greaseproof paper, so why not double the recipe? You can then take out as many as you need at a time even for an American style breakfast with maple syrup and bacon.

Pappardelle with Mussels and Roquefort

Ingredients

600g	mussels
2	shallots, finely chopped
	olive oil
2	parsley stalks
80ml	white wine
200g	dried pappardelle pasta
150g	roquefort
150ml	double cream
	chervil or flat parsley for garnishing

Serves 4

This is a simple recipe and one that won't be beyond the ability of most home cooks.

It's so salty and so savoury: I love the rich combination.

Pick through the mussels checking over for any that may be open.

Remove any beards and barnacles and give them a good wash in water.

In a suitable pan sweat the shallot in a little oil, add the mussels and shake them around the pan. Pour in the white wine and add the parsley stalks, cover with a lid and cook until the mussels are open.

Tip them into a colander over a bowl to retain all the juice. Once cool, pass the cooking juice through a sieve, leaving behind any sediment.

Open the mussels one by one and remove the mussel from the shell.

Drop them back into the cooking juice. Keep a dozen or so shells for decorating the plate at the time of serving.

Serving:

Fill a deep saucepan with water and pour a drop of oil into it, bring it to the boil with a pinch of salt. Add the pasta and cook it al dente.

In a separate pan bring the mussel juice back to the boil, reduce by a half and then add the double cream. Bring it back to the boil and then add 100g of the cheese.

Whisk it together to become smooth. Drain the pasta and then roll it into the sauce. Divide into 4 bowls, decorate with the shells, crumble the remaining Roquefort on top and garnish with a little chervil or flat parsley.

Chef's note:

It's always good to buy a few extra mussels as inevitably some will have broken shells or be open.

These should be discarded as the mussel will already be dead.

Hot Smoked Salmon with Crab & Aïoli

Ingredients

4	160g salmon fillets

Brine

650ml	water
100g	salt
70g	sugar
2	juniper berries, crushed
2	cloves
2	black peppercorns, crushed

Crab

1	cock crab

Aïoli

2	medium baked potatoes giving 200g of smooth purée
125ml	warmed milk infused with a pinch of saffron
2	cloves of garlic crushed with a pinch of salt
150ml	good quality extra virgin olive oil

Serves 4

Bring all the brine ingredients to the boil and leave to cool. Keep refrigerated until needed.

Cook the crab and then leave to cool in its cooking liquor. Once cold, pick and then check the crab meat thoroughly for small pieces of shell.

In a moderate oven dry out the crab shells with a good spoon of tomato purée, a carrot, onion, garlic and thyme.

Once dried place in a suitable container and then cover with a light olive oil, leave to infuse for at least 24 hours.

Pass through a fine muslin leaving behind any sediment and keep refrigerated

For the aïoli, in a suitable bowl place the potato purée, whisk in half of the milk and the garlic then gradually whisk in the olive oil.

When the mixture becomes too thick to whisk add the remainder of the milk and then the rest of the oil. Season and reserve until needed.

Cooking and serving:

Take the salmon fillets and place into the brine for 5 minutes. Whilst this is brining light the smoker and when the 5 minutes is up dry and then place the salmon into the smoker.

Depending on the heat and the required cooking degree the salmon should be ready in about 5-7 minutes.

Place a circle of aïoli in the middle of the plate with the salmon on top, dress the plate with salad, herbs and the flaked crab, and also place a good quenelle of the crab on top of the salmon.

Lastly drizzle some of the crab infused olive oil around.

Chef's note:

If you're in a hurry for the brine halve the water in the recipe and once boiled add the equivalent of the missing water in ice cubes.

Fillet of Cod with Sea Salt, Crushed Potatoes & Chorizo with Tomato & Thyme Vinaigrette

Ingredients

1	fillet of cod weighing at least 600g
150g	tomatoes, skinned and de-seeded
6	sprigs of thyme
100ml	tomato juice
10ml	sherry vinegar
75ml	pomace olive oil
12	new potatoes
60g	raw chorizo sausage
300ml	milk for poaching the fish
1	bay leaf

Tomato vinaigrette

150g	tomatoes, skinned and de-seeded
5	sprigs of thyme
100ml	tomato juice
10ml	sherry vinegar

Serves 4

This dish is the taste of Spain and Portugal. However, as much as I love to see the salt cod hanging up or neatly stacked in the fish market, this version is all together milder and more sophisticated.

Take the fillet of cod, skin and then pin bone it.

On a suitable tray cover it with sea salt and leave it in the fridge for 45 minutes.

Lightly rinse off the salt with cold water. Cut the cod into 4 portions allowing 150g per person.

For the tomato vinaigrette combine all of the above in a liquidiser, season, blend and gently add the pomace olive oil.

Pass and place in fridge until required.

Serving:

Cook a dozen new potatoes in their skins in boiling water with a pinch of salt, once cooked refresh with cold water and then peel them.

When needed put a good splash of olive oil in a suitable pan and add the diced raw chorizo sausage.

Once the oil is released add the potatoes crushing them in your hand at the same time.

Poach the portions of cod in milk with the thyme and bay leaf, covered with greaseproof paper.

Halfway through cooking turn them over to give an even cooking.

Depending on the thickness of the cod fillet it will take approximately 6 minutes to cook.

Place the potato and chorizo in the middle of the plate.

Mix the vinaigrette a little before pouring around the potato.

Place the cod on top of the potato, sprinkle with sea salt and garnish with some rocket leaves.

Monkfish Loin wrapped in Prosciutto Ham, Potato Purée, Orange & Balsamic Sauce

Ingredients

Monkfish

2	medium sized monkfish, giving 4 fillets of approximately 160g each
8	slices of prosciutto ham
8	leaves of sage, blanched in boiling water

Orange and balsamic sauce

Reduce together

150ml	orange juice
40ml	fish stock
10g	sugar
1	dessert spoon of aged balsamic vinegar

When syrupy add:

150ml	double cream

Serves 4

To add to the saltimbocca theme, I like to use a little blanched sage in this dish. It's a perfect balance of sweet and savoury with great acidity.

Trim the monkfish fillets well and remove any membrane or sinew from the fillets. Lay a piece of cling film flat onto a work surface.

Lay two slices of prosciutto ham side by side onto the cling film.

Now lay the monkfish fillet onto the ham with two leaves of blanched sage.

Fold over the cling film and then tightly roll each fillet in the film, giving a sausage-like shape and tying both ends.

Follow the reduction instructions for the sauce, adding double cream when a syrup forms.

Once again cook for about a minute until the sauce is slightly thickening. Pass through a fine sieve, season with a pinch of salt and reserve.

Serving:

Poach the fillets of monkfish in a pan of simmering water for approximately 8-10 minutes.

The monkfish should be warm through. Use a needle or skewer to test the temperature.

Prepare the garnish of orange segments, oyster mushrooms, French beans, leaf spinach and potato purée.

Once the monkfish is cooked, remove from the water, unwrap the cling film, pat dry with kitchen roll and then lightly pan fry in olive oil to colour the ham.

Carefully put the potato purée into the centre of the plate and then place the warmed garnish around the plate.

Slice the monkfish into three, at an angle, this will give the dish some height.

Place the pieces of fish around the potato and finally gently pour the sauce around.

Fillets of Red Mullet with Bouillon

Ingredients

2	450g fish giving four fillets of 120g each

Bouillion

400g	red mullet bones and heads
300g	onion
300g	carrots
2	cloves garlic
2	sticks celery
50g	tomato purée
160ml	white wine
	Ricard (optional)
1l	fish stock
	saffron
	salt and pepper

Garnish

8	new potatoes cooked in their skins and then peeled
40g	samphire
2	carrots, into parisienne balls
12	mange tout

Tempura batter

50g	rice flour
25g	corn flour
5g	baking powder
15ml	white wine vinegar
65ml	water, from the fridge
	salt and pepper

Serves 4

To further enhance these wonderful Mediterranean flavours and to add another dimension, serve it with a rouille or aïoli.

Take the two 450g fish and remove the fillets. Clean the red mullet bones to remove any blood and also remove the gills from the heads.

Leave to clean in running water until the water is clear. Drain them in a colander and shake to remove any excess water. Take two pans with a drop of olive oil in both. In one, cook off the mullet bones and in the other cook together the vegetables and garlic, adding the tomato purée a little later.

De-glaze the mullet pan with the white wine and add this to the pan of vegetables. If you are feeling a little French you can add a drop of Ricard at this point. Add the fish stock, a pinch of saffron and a little seasoning.

Leave to cook on a gentle simmer for a couple of hours, skimming off any fat/oil regularly.

Once cooked remove from the heat, blend with a hand blender and then pass everything through a fine sieve. Discard the pulp and reduce the liquid by about a third. Correct the seasoning and keep to one side.

Season and, in a non-stick pan, cook the red mullet fillets starting with the skin side down. Re-heat the bouillon.

Top, tail and then cut each mange tout into three or four long strips.

Flour them and then dip into the tempura batter - whisked together from ingredients - and deep fry in oil at 180ºc. Season once cooked.

Slice and re-heat the potatoes in boiling water and place the fish on top of them.

Arrange the samphire and carrot balls around and pour on the bouillon, finally top the dish with the tempura of mange tout.

Turbot Cooked on the Bone with Sorrel Sauce

Ingredients

4 x	180g pieces of turbot cut on the bone
120g	brown shrimps
50g	unsalted butter
12	new potatoes
1	small bunch of chives
8	radishes, halved
1	granny smith apple, cut into batons with the skin on
	red amaranth for garnish

Sorrel sauce

25g	finely chopped shallot
30ml	white wine
60ml	fish stock
120ml	double cream
10g	sorrel torn into 1 inch pieces

Serves 4

When I became Sous-Chef at The Waterside Inn in 1986, I was privileged to spend ten days at Troisgros, in Roanne, as a Stagiere. Sorrel Sauce will always remind me of that. This isn't their recipe but it's a close second place.

For a perfect result, start the cooking of the sauce and turbot at the same time.

For the sauce, put the shallot and white wine into a small pan and reduce the wine until almost dry, then add the fish stock, reduce by a half and then add the double cream, re-boil to thicken a little, season and pass through a fine sieve onto the torn sorrel.

Seal the pieces of turbot in an oven proof non-stick pan with a drop of olive oil with a knob of butter.

Once nicely coloured, place it into a pre-heated oven at 180°c for 10 minutes, turning it once half way through cooking.

With a few minutes to go add the brown shrimps to the pan.

To make sure the fish is cooked make a small cut along the bone of one of the pieces and ease the meat away to check.

Drain the fish on a paper towel before serving.

In a saucepan of water add a pinch of salt, once boiling add the halved radishes and a minute later add the pre-cooked potatoes.

Serving:

Pour a little of the sauce onto the plate and place the fish on top of this, carefully put the shrimps to one side and the radishes on the other.

Drain the new potatoes and roll them in the remaining butter with the snipped chives.

Place these around the fish and top the dish off with the raw apple and the red amaranth.

Fillet of Sea Bass with Jerusalem Artichoke Purée, Roasted Garlic, Butter Beans, Flageolets & Red Wine Jus

Ingredients

4   *150g fillets of sea bass (pin boned and scaled, but with the skin on and scored to prevent curling when cooking)*

Jerusalem artichoke purée

200g   *Jerusalem artichokes, peeled and roughly chopped*
150ml   *double cream*

Beans and flageolets

100g   *dried butter beans*
100g   *dried flageolets*

Roast garlic

1   *head of garlic*
      olive oil
      sea salt

Red wine jus

200ml   *red wine*
200ml   *veal stock*
1   *sprig of thyme*
50g   *sliced shallot*

Serves 4

I love the earthy flavour of Jerusalem artichokes, which combine wonderfully with sea bass. A lovely glossy and rich red wine sauce finishes off this dish.

Cook the artichokes in water with a pinch of salt, (this will take at least an hour). Drain well and return them to the pan to lose any remaining moisture. Cover with the cream, bring back to the boil and reduce slightly, then blend, season and if necessary pass through a sieve.

Soak the beans and flageolets overnight. Rinse and cook them separately in water with a little salt and a sprig of thyme. They will take at least an hour to cook and should be tender to eat but not falling apart.

Break apart a head of garlic and place in tin foil with a little olive oil and sea salt. Scrunch up the top of the tin foil so as to create a little parcel and place on a bed of sea salt in a suitable baking tray. This prevents the garlic inside the foil from burning.

Bake at 180°c for approximately 20 minutes, the garlic should be getting soft by that point. Peel the skin away from the garlic and reserve.

Make a reduction of 200ml red wine with a good sprig of thyme and 50g of sliced shallot. Once almost dry add 200ml veal stock and reduce to a near syrupy consistency. Pass before using.

Serving:

Place in a large non-stick pan over a medium-high heat. Once the pan is scorching hot, add the sea bass fillets, skin-side down, reduce heat and cook until the skin is crispy, about 3 minutes.

Turn the fillets over, season, and then cook on this side until the fish is delicately cooked through - no longer than a couple of minutes. Rest the fish in the pan - any residual heat from the pan should finish the cooking process effectively.

Re-heat the beans and flageolets in a little double cream, boil, season and place in the middle of the plate. Place the fish on top and then neatly dot the purée in 3 areas and in between serve some sautéed spinach, sun dried tomatoes and pieces of the roasted garlic. Gently pour a little sauce over the fish, and garnish with deep fried rocket leaves.

Halibut Fillet with Potato Crust, Cider Cream Sauce

Ingredients

4	150g halibut fillets
275ml	medium-sweet cider
1	pinch of sugar
150ml	veal stock
200ml	double cream
1	large potato
2	egg yolks
1	Cox's apple
	edible seaweed

Braised lettuce

2	little gem lettuce
100ml	cider

Serves 4

We always joke that this dish is our version of fish and chips.

Starting with the potato crust, peel and cut the potato into matchsticks and blanch in oil at 110°c until soft, without colour.

Leave to cool. Once ready mix together with the yolks and a pinch of salt. Pat a little flour onto the presentation side of the fillet and then place on the potato.

For the sauce, reduce the cider by two thirds with a pinch of sugar, then add the veal stock and reduce by half.

Add the double cream and leave to cook until a good consistency and giving 180ml of sauce, then season.

With a parisienne spoon make 24 apple balls and at the last minute add the apple balls to the sauce and gently reheat.

Now, remove a couple of outer leaves from the lettuce and cut them in half. Colour in a hot pan moistened with olive oil. Once coloured, season and pour in the cider.

Cover with greaseproof paper and cook in a pre-heated oven at 140°C for around 5 minutes. Before serving cut an upside down "V" out of the core.

Serving:

Pan fry the halibut with the potato-side down on a gentle heat for approximately 5 minutes.

Make sure the potato doesn't colour too much. Turn over the fish and cook for a couple of minutes on the other side.

To check if the fish is cooked through, insert a thin skewer into the thickest part of the fish for a few seconds and then touch the skewer to your lip.

If it is hot, the fish is ready. Place the fish in the centre of the plate with the lettuce and a little edible seaweed.

If you're lucky enough to have any monk's beard or samphire, use to compliment this dish.

Pour a little sauce around the fish and serve immediately.

Stuffed Saddle of Rabbit, Parsley Risotto & Spring Vegetables

Ingredients

2	1.5kg rabbits, if you wish to use the legs for the stuffing, or 2 saddles of rabbit.
100g	pig's caul
200g	chicken (optional)
1	egg
100ml	double cream
	salt and cayenne pepper

Sauce

1	onion
1	carrot
1	celery stick
1tsp	tomato purée
	splash of white wine
1	bunch of tarragon or thyme
500ml	veal stock

Risotto

175g	carnaroli risotto rice
100ml	white wine
50g	finely chopped onion
1tbsp	olive oil
600ml	chicken stock
50g	finely grated Parmesan cheese
	fresh parsley

Serves 4

Remove the offal from the rabbits, retaining the liver. Remove the shoulders and legs leaving the two loins intact on the bone giving the saddle.

At this point, carefully de-bone the saddles and refrigerate. Dice the livers and quickly sauté in a very hot pan, drain on a piece of absorbent paper, cool and reserve.

Make a forcemeat from 200g meat (either from the rabbit legs or chicken breast) and 100g pork fat.

Mince together and add a whole egg, place over ice and beat in 100ml double cream. Season with salt and a pinch of cayenne pepper. Gently add the livers and adjust the seasoning.

Open the saddles and fill with a good spoon of forcemeat and fold the belly over to close the saddle. Be careful not to have too much of the belly overlapping (trim if necessary). Wrap each saddle in pig's caul and tie lightly with string.

To make the sauce, sweat the shoulders and other trimmings with onion, celery and carrot and add a tsp of tomato purée.

Once coloured de-glaze with a good splash of white wine and add a small bunch of tarragon or thyme. Bring to the boil and simmer for at least an hour.

Once the stock has cooked, pass and reduce and then finally mix it half and half with veal stock.

For the risotto, heat the oil in a pan. Sweat the onions in the oil so they are soft but not coloured. Add the rice to the pan and stir with a spatula until the rice is coated with the oil. Add the white wine and bring it to the boil, don't stir the rice until the wine is boiling.

Then ladle by ladle, add the stock and keep stirring until each ladleful is absorbed.

Keep stirring the stock in until the rice is tender but still with a slight resistance to the bite - this should take about 15-18 minutes.

Remove the risotto from the heat and finish with a good knob of butter or a splash of double cream, the parmesan and a dessert spoon of chopped parsley.

Cooking and serving:

Gently seal the saddles in a pan of hot oil add a good knob of butter and place into a pre-heated oven at 180°c. After 10 minutes, reduce the temperature to 160°c for a further 15 minutes, remove and leave to rest for a good 10 minutes before carving.

Sauté together some lovely spring vegetables, peas, broad beans, baby carrots and, of course, some morel mushrooms. Pour a little of the sauce around and serve at once.

Chef's note:

For this dish I prefer to use a farmed rabbit rather than a wild one as they can be smaller and sometimes badly shot.

Chicken in a Brick with Spice & Yoghurt

Ingredients

1 x	1.7kg chicken
1	lemon, into juice and zest, keep the empty lemon shell for flavouring in the cavity of the chicken
50g	tomato purée
10g	garam masala
200g	natural yoghurt
1	sprig of fresh coriander

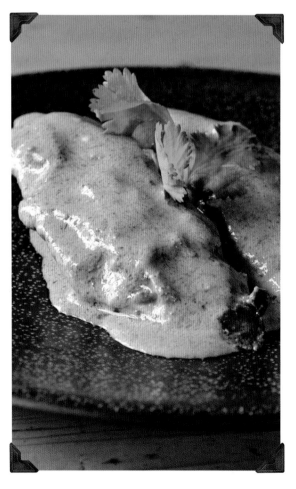

Serves 4

This has all the flavour of a traditional tandoor cooked chicken. I believe there was a time when High Street shops were full of Chicken Bricks, though they seem to be harder to find these days. If one isn't available to you a good pan with a tight fitting lid will be almost as good.

Trim off the wings, and remove the wishbone from the chicken.

Make a paste from the lemon juice, zest, tomato purée, garam masala, 3 pinches of salt and 100g of the yoghurt.

Rub the chicken with this paste and place the two half lemon shells inside the body cavity. Leave to marinade/infuse for 24 hours in the fridge.

To avoid cracking, soak the chicken brick in cold water 15 minutes before needed.

Season the inside of the chicken with salt and place it into the brick, close with the lid.

Place the chicken brick onto a tray and into a cold oven. Turn the oven on to 180°c. and cook for 1hr 45 minutes.

Remove the chicken from the brick and leave it to rest before cutting. Drain and pass the cooking juices through a fine sieve and skim off any excess fat. Stir in the remaining yoghurt (100g) into the juices and about 2g of chopped coriander leaves. Portion the chicken and spoon the dressing over the top.

Chef's note:

This dish is lovely served with some fragrant rice and naan bread.

If any chicken is left over it will be just as delicious the next day accompanied by some raita.

Breast of Corn-Fed Chicken with Truffled Sausage, Potato Purée, Leeks, Thyme Jus

Ingredients

9	breasts of corn-fed chicken, 1 is used for making the mousse for the sausage
1	egg white
1	whole egg
250ml	double cream
50g	white breadcrumbs
5g	chopped black truffle or chopped herbs

Thyme jus

25g	shallots (peeled and sliced)
60ml	white wine
8	sticks of thyme
350ml	chicken stock
175ml	veal stock

Potato purée with leeks

4	large baking potatoes, 250g each, scored around the middle
2	leeks, 150g each
400ml	double cream
80g	butter

Vegetables

1	courgette, thinly sliced on a mandolin into 8 slices
200g	curly kale
1	large butternut squash

Serves 8

Corn fed chicken breasts will lift this dish to a different level. This recipe can easily be halved if needed.

To make chicken mousse sausages, skin and remove any bone and sinew from one of the chicken breasts. Place into a food processor with a pinch of salt and the egg white. Blend to form a smooth paste.

Pass this through a drum sieve and place into a bowl over ice then gently beat in the double cream in 20ml measures.

Check the seasoning and add a little chopped truffle or chopped herbs. Roll in cling film tightly to form sausage shapes and poach in water that is just below boiling (80°c) for 7-8 minutes.

Leave to cool and set in the fridge before unwrapping and coating in flour, egg and breadcrumbs.

For the thyme jus, place the shallots, white wine and thyme into a pan and reduce until almost dry. Add the chicken stock and reduce by half. Finally add the veal stock and reduce again to a good consistency. Pass, season and reserve.

Now, bake the potatoes in their skins in a preheated oven at 200°c for approximately 1 hour. Wash the leeks and cut them into 2cm dice.

Blanch the leeks in boiling salted water, retaining a bit of a crunch. Refresh in cold water and drain. When the potatoes are cooked, halve them to remove the flesh and pass through a drum sieve or a potato ricer.

In a suitable pan boil the cream and add the potato. Whisk the mix until smooth, add the butter and lastly the leeks. Season and reserve.

Peel the tubular end of the butternut squash. Cut it in half length wise and cut 12 semi-circles from each half, giving 24 pieces. Shape into crescents with the aid of a cutter if necessary.

Pan fry the crescents in a little oil and a knob of butter, colouring gently. Grill one strip of courgette per portion and lightly flash fry the curly kale.

Serving:

Start the chicken breasts in a pan on the stove skin side down and then cook in a pre-heated oven at 180°c for approximately 20 minutes. Gently pan fry the bread-crumbed chicken sausage.

Line a 7cm ring or cutter with the grilled courgette and then fill with the hot potato and leek mixture.

Carefully slice the chicken and arrange it neatly on the plate with the squash and kale. Cut the sausage in half at an angle, and then gently pour a little sauce around.

Chef's note:

A great way of checking the cooking of the chicken is to lift the under fillet of the breast. Once the chicken has changed from its natural opaque colour to white it will be cooked.

Poussin with Peppers, Potato Rösti & Tarragon Jus

Ingredients

4	poussin
2	large potatoes
1	red pepper
1	yellow pepper
200g	leaf spinach

Jus

15g	shallots, peeled and sliced
30ml	white wine
200ml	chicken stock
100ml	veal stock
4	sprigs of tarragon, cut 6 of the best leaves into dice
	salt and pepper

Serves 4

Remove the legs and first two wing joints from the birds.

Take out the wishbones and then with a pair of poultry scissors cut from the rear end to the neck leaving the two breasts still on the bone.

Be careful to leave the wing bone attached to the crown.

Trim off any excess skin and chop off the very tip of the wing joint with a heavy knife.

Divide the legs into thighs and drumsticks, keeping the thighs to cook with the crowns.

If you don't have any chicken stock to hand, make a little stock with the carcasses and drumsticks.

For the peppers, remove the stalks, cut in half and remove the seeds. Place onto a tray, season and moisten with a little olive oil. Cover tightly with tin foil to create some steam and place into a pre-heated oven at 160°c.

After about 45 minutes you should be able to peel the skin away from the peppers. Once skinned cut them into long strips.

To make the jus, place the shallots, white wine and tarragon in a pan and reduce until almost dry. Add the chicken stock, cook slowly and reduce the liquid by half. Add the veal stock and reduce again to a sauce-like consistency. Pass through a fine sieve, season and reserve.

Add the remaining diced tarragon just prior to serving.

Rösti potatoes

Peel and finely shred two potatoes on a mandolin or grater. Season with salt and squeeze out as much water as possible. In individual pans pour a drop of oil, divide the potato into the pans and spread the potato evenly, fry until golden. If you prefer a thicker rösti use an extra potato and pop the röstis into the oven with a knob of butter, to help cook them through.

Cooking and serving:

Season and seal the poussin on all sides in a hot pan, place them skin side down with the thighs and place in a pre-heated oven at 180°c for 25 minutes, turning once during cooking. Whilst the poussin is resting, de-vein and wash 200g of leaf spinach, dry in a salad spinner and sauté in olive oil, season to taste - re-heat the peppers in the oven.

After 5 minutes, when the poussin have rested, turn them skin side down and make a small cut between the wing and the carcass revealing two bones on the carcass.

Push them up and remove, then holding the flat edge of a knife across the breasts gently pull up the breast bone to remove it in one piece. Trim the knuckle bones on the thighs and dress on the plates with the röstis, spinach and peppers. Finally pour a little of the sauce around and serve.

Confit of Duck, Lime & Honey Glaze

Ingredients

4	good sized duck legs
750ml	vegetable oil
150g	table salt
50g	curly kale, de-veined, and a vegetable garnish such as courgette, baby onions and cocotte potatoes.

For the glaze

½	lime juice and zest
15g	grated fresh root ginger
1	pinch of ground ginger
100g	honey
100ml	olive oil
1	dessert spoon of lime cordial
1	pinch of salt

Serves 4

This is the classic confit. I prefer to use the legs rather than the breasts, which can be a little dry.

The lime glaze cuts through the duck and gives this dish a real zing. Warm the honey and add to this all the other ingredients. Bring it together with the aid of a hand blender.

With a heavy knife chop the knuckles off the legs and then heavily salt the duck legs along with fresh thyme. Cover and keep refrigerated for 2 hours.

When the time is up, rinse them in cold water then place into a deep tray and cover with all the oil, placing the skin side up. Remember that during the cooking process the legs will give up some fat.

Uncover the duck legs and then put the tray into a pre-heated oven at 140°c for approximately 2 hours. During this time, the duck legs should begin to take some colour. Once cooked, they should be soft to the touch.

Leave to cool in the fat but remove them before the fat sets.

On a baking sheet place a square of greaseproof paper and onto that place the duck legs skin side up. Coat the legs with half of the lime glaze and bake in a pre-warmed oven at 180°c for 20 minutes or until hot.

Cook the curly kale in a pan of seasoned boiling water with a knob of butter. Place the kale onto the plate and the duck on top.

Neatly arrange the remaining vegetables onto the plate and lastly add the remaining glaze.

Chef's note:

The remaining fat from the confit, once passed while still warm, can be re-used or is perfect for roasting potatoes.

Chopping off the knuckles before cooking will leave the drumstick bone clean, giving a better presentation.

Breast of Duck with Orange Sauce, Pommes Berny

Ingredients

4	240g duck breasts trimmed, small fillet removed and the skin lightly scored, giving a net weight of 185g each.
3	baking potatoes
	salt
	knob of butter
10g	chopped truffle
20g	white breadcrumbs
10g	nibbed almonds
10g	flaked almonds

Sauce

40ml	orange juice
25g	caster sugar
50ml	red wine vinegar
200ml	veal stock
	Grand-Marnier
	lemon juice (optional)

Garnish

2	beetroots
2	golden beetroots
8	pieces of tenderstem broccoli

Serves 4

It was my honour to cook this dish for The Great British Chefs Dinner in aid of the NSPCC in 2014. Pommes berny is the French name for these wonderful potatoes.

Score around three baking potatoes and place on a baking tray on a bed of salt in a pre-heated oven at 200°c for an hour or until soft.

Once cooked, remove the flesh and pass it through a sieve. Season and add a good knob of butter (if the potato is wet be careful not to add too much).

Add 10g of chopped truffle and mix and roll into balls. A portion of potatoes should be 2 x 30g balls.

These are then bread-crumbed in a mixture of 20g white breadcrumbs, 10g nibbed almonds and 10g flaked almonds.

When needed deep fry in oil at 180°c until golden and heated through.

For the sauce, cook together the orange juice, sugar and vinegar until it has reduced and become syrupy.

Add the veal stock. Cook again until a good consistency and to add a luxurious taste.

Finish with a drop of Grand Marnier. If you prefer, a sharper sauce, a squeeze of lemon juice can be added at this point.

To garnish, cut and shape the beetroots into segments: three of each per portion. Roast them in the oven in oil with a good sprig of thyme.

Serving:

Season the duck and cook in a dry frying pan, two thirds on the skin side and one third on the flesh side, until pink. Enough fat will come out of the duck to stop it sticking to the pan.

Leave to rest before slicing into 6 even slices. Neatly arrange them on the plate and garnish with tenderstem broccoli and the deep fried potatoes.

Finally pour the sauce around.

Suprême of Guinea Fowl with Morel Cream Sauce

Ingredients

2	whole guinea fowl
1	carrot
1	stick of celery
1	onion
1	garlic bulb
1	bay leaf
2	cloves

Mousse

2	thighs, from the whole fowl
1	egg white
125ml	double cream
	salt and pepper

Cannelloni

125g	00 pasta flour
1	egg yolk
1	whole egg
1	tsp olive oil
1	pinch of salt

Sauce

50g	morels
25ml	white wine
140ml	guinea fowl stock
60ml	veal stock
100ml	double cream

Serves 4

Writing this book has made me realise how long this sauce has been with me... since 1978 at The Portman Hotel.

Break down the birds into breasts and legs and then further divide the legs into thighs and drumsticks.

Make a stock by covering the carcasses and drumsticks with water and add carrot, celery, onion, garlic, a bay leaf and a couple of cloves.

Once boiled, reduce the heat to a simmer and cook the stock for 30 minutes. Pass through a fine sieve and reduce gently by two thirds, skimming from time to time.

Pass again and retain to use in the sauce.

For the mousse, skin and trim any fat from the thighs and remove the thigh bones. Dice the meat and blend to a paste in a food processor with the egg white and a pinch of salt. Rub it through a drum sieve.

Place the paste in a bowl on ice and gradually beat in the double cream in about 20ml measures. Once incorporated, season and reserve.

To confit the thighs, salt them for 40 minutes and rinse them under cold water. Submerge them in vegetable oil in a deep pan and place in a pre-heated oven for approximately 2 hours at 120ºc.

Once cooked, cool and then remove from the oil. Take off the skin and flake the meat away from the bone, being careful not to keep any cartilage.

Cannelloni pasta is made by combining the flour, salt and eggs in a food processor and then add the oil, drop by drop, to form a crumbly texture.

Form the dough by hand into a flat rectangular shape, cling film and refrigerate to rest for a couple of hours.

Combine the flaked meat with the mousse and transfer to a piping bag.

Roll out the pasta by putting it through a pasta roller, decreasing the thickness each time and finishing when it is as thin as possible.

Lay the sheet of pasta onto a work surface dusted with flour and pipe the filling in a line along the centre.

Brush the far edge with egg wash, fold the pasta over the filling trimming any excess. Roll into a long sausage shape sealing it with egg wash.

Cut into four 12cm batons and wrap each one tightly in cling film to form the cannelloni and refrigerate until needed.

continues over

Now, lightly pan fry the breasts in oil, giving a golden colour to the skin.

A good test to see if it is cooked is to lift the small fillet on the underside, the meat should be firm and no longer opaque. Drop the cannelloni into a pan of simmering water and cook for about 8 minutes.

Once cooked unwrap the cling film with the aid of a pair of scissors and roll the cannelloni in a pan of foaming butter. Before serving cut off the ends to neaten them up with a sharp knife.

The cooking of the breast should take no longer than 8-10 minutes so these two elements should be ready at the same time.

When making the sauce, if you are using dried morels soak overnight before using. Other wild mushrooms can be used but I would choose a type of mushroom with a delicate flavour.

Once the guinea fowl is cooked, swill the pan round with a little white wine, pass into a clean pan and add the morels, the reduced stock and the veal stock.

Bring to the boil and simmer for a couple of minutes before adding the cream.

Boil again, season as required, and pour gently over the guinea fowl.

Garnish with some lovely, colourful vegetables such as asparagus and French beans.

Pork Fillet with Potato, Prosciutto & Parmesan Gratin

Ingredients

16	60g pork medallions

Potato gratin

6	large potatoes
6	cloves garlic
150ml	milk
275ml	double cream
12	slices prosciutto
100g	parmesan

Garnish

1	red pepper
1	yellow pepper
1	courgette
400g	leaf spinach

Marjoram jus

50g	shallot
1	bunch of marjoram
100ml	white wine
400ml	veal stock

Serves 8

This dish includes 1980s retro presentation!

For the potato gratin, peel and crush the garlic, place into a pan with the milk and cream and bring to the boil. Peel and finely slice the potatoes, divide them into four even piles to ensure even layers when assembling the gratin.

Place a circle of baking parchment in a suitable pan and lay in the potatoes with three even layers of prosciutto and Parmesan interspersed.

Pour through a sieve a little of the cream onto each layer and season.

Before baking, place on the stove on a gentle heat for 5 minutes to start colouring and then bake in the oven at 180°c for up to 1½ hours.

Check the cooking by inserting a needle or skewer into the gratin.

Once cooked, press with a weight until cold.

At the time of serving, cut into segments and re-heat in the oven.

Make the garnish by de-veining and washing the spinach. Dry in a salad spinner and sauté in olive oil. To add a garlicky flavour, pierce a clove of garlic onto a fork and stir the spinach with this during cooking. Season to taste.

Cut the other vegetables neatly into squares and also sauté in olive oil.

To make the marjoram jus, slice the shallot and place in a pan with the wine and marjoram and reduce until almost dry.

Add the stock, bring to the boil and leave to cook gently.

Once this has reached a light sauce consistency, season and pass.

Serving:

Pan fry the pork medallions, giving a good colour.

Neatly arrange the diced vegetables and place a slice of gratin onto the plate.

Drain the spinach well, make a ball of it on top of the medallions and finally top with a little of the sauce.

Chef's note:

I believe pork should be cooked through but not overcooked.

As an alternative potato dish make a root vegetable gratin using, for example, one third beetroot and two thirds sweet potato.

Pork Belly with Braised Red Cabbage & Apple Compôte

Ingredients

2.8kg	pork belly on the bone or 2.2kg boned
1	carrot
1	onion
1	celery
1	bay leaf
4	cloves
1	star anise

Red cabbage

1	red cabbage, finely shredded
100g	soft dark brown sugar
150ml	red wine vinegar

Apple compôte

4	Granny Smith apples
4tbsp	caster sugar

Serves 8

The classic! Our recipe differs from many as the pork is poached prior to roasting. This makes it extremely tender and loses some of the fat from a notoriously fatty joint. It also speeds up cooking time on the day.

De-bone, trim and skin the belly. Cover and poach in water with a carrot, onion, celery, bay leaf, 4 cloves and a star anise. Leave to gently simmer for 3-4 hours.

Leave it to cool in the liquor. Once cold remove from the liquor, wrap in cling film and press it between two trays weighted down. Refrigerate until needed and then cut the belly into 8 even batons.

For the sauce, pass and reduce the cooking liquor, skimming off the fat (there will be lots).

Once it is boiling mix it 50-50 with veal stock and reduce to a good consistency. Finish with a tablespoon of clear honey to add a hint of sweetness.

For the red cabbage, boil together the vinegar and sugar. Then add the red cabbage, cook until tender (at least an hour) but don't let the cabbage boil dry. If there is too much liquid left, reduce it and add it back to the cabbage.

To make the apple compôte, peel and dice the apple. Cook it with the sugar and a drop of water in a suitable pan with a circle of greaseproof paper on top until it is soft but still keeps its shape.

Serving:

Place the pork skin side down onto a baking sheet lined with baking parchment. Place into a pre-heated oven at 180°c for about 20 minutes.

Turn the pork once towards the end of cooking. Re-heat the cabbage and the apple and dress neatly on a plate. Pour a little sauce over the pork, but not over the apple and serve immediately.

Chef's note:

Any rib bones will be excellent for sticky spare ribs!

Lamb Confit Suet Pudding

Ingredients

1kg	middle neck lamb fillets
450g	baby onions

Rosemary jus

25g	shallot
25g	carrot
1	good sprig of rosemary, picked
120ml	white wine
600ml	lamb or veal stock

Suet pastry

600g	self raising flour
80g	suet or lard
80g	margarine
320ml	water
1	pinch mustard powder
	salt & pepper

Serves 8

Full of wintry goodness, there's nothing like an early supper in front of the fire.

For confit lamb, salt the middle lamb neck fillets for 45 minutes, rinse and then cook gently in a deep pan of oil or rendered lamb fat in a pre-heated oven at 120°c until they are soft.

This will take a good couple of hours. They may need covering with tin foil towards the end of cooking as they shouldn't become too dark.

Around 20 minutes before being ready add the peeled baby onions to the pan and gently cook them.

This long process can easily be done the day before.

The puddings have a two-part process. Start with a rosemary jus.

Sauté the shallot and carrots, de-glaze with the white wine add the rosemary and reduce.

Add the stock, bring to the boil and leave to cook gently.

Once this has reached a light sauce consistency, season and pass.

Take a third of this jus and thicken with a little corn flour this will be the jus to go inside the puddings.

Now, for the suet pastry, rub together the flour, mustard powder, salt, pepper, lard and margarine and then bind with the water.

Roll out on a floured surface and cut out 8 circles, keep the trimmings for the lids.

Butter 8 individual moulds and then roll and line them with the suet pastry and fill with cubes of the lamb and onion confit.

Cover with the rosemary sauce, which has been thickened with the corn flour.

Roll out the 8 lids and close the puddings. Cover with buttered greaseproof paper and then tin foil.

Cook in a bain-marie in a pre-heated oven at 160°c for 2¼ hours.

Serving:

When the puddings are cooked, savour the aroma and serve with buttered new potatoes, shaped carrots and any leftover onions.

Cover the pudding with sauce and eat immediately.

Chef's note:

In preference use an individual pudding mould 8.5cm in diameter.

And 'thanks Ma' for all those steak and kidney puddings.

Loin of Lamb with Sweetbreads, Aubergine Purée & Boulangère Potatoes

Ingredients

Lamb loin

1	short saddle of lamb, the two loins will give four portions
50ml	white wine
100ml	lamb stock
150g	lamb sweetbreads
25g	unsalted butter
	spring vegetables as garnish

Boulangère potatoes with confit

250g	lamb breast flank, from the short saddle
10g	salt
100ml	vegetable oil
1	small stick of rosemary
1	clove garlic
1	medium onion
3	large potatoes, 250g each
150ml	lamb stock

Aubergine purée

1	medium aubergine, 350g
2	cloves of garlic
½	teaspoon of cumin seeds
50ml	double cream
	olive oil
	salt and pepper

Serves 4

The potato dish is almost a meal on its own. It's a "deluxe" Lancashire Hot Pot!

Remove the two loins from the saddle and trim them being careful to remove the sinew.

You can, if you like, leave a little of the fat on which will melt away slightly during the cooking.

Soak the sweetbreads overnight in water to purge any blood from them.

Trim the lamb breast, being careful to remove as much sinew as possible.

Salt for 25 minutes before rinsing under the cold tap. Place them into a suitable deep tray.

Add the rosemary and garlic and then cover with the vegetable oil.

Cover the dish with tin foil and cook it in a pre-heated oven at 140°c for 2½ to 3 hours until very soft.

Discard the garlic and rosemary and leave it to cool before removing from the fat and flaking it between your fingers.

Peel and finely slice the onion, cook it in a frying pan slowly so that it is soft but without colour.

Peel and thinly slice the potatoes. Line a suitable deep dish with greaseproof paper and layer in the potatoes, the onion and the shredded confit.

Season a little between the layers bearing in mind that the confit is naturally salty.

Pour in the stock and then cover the top with greaseproof paper and bake in a pre-heated oven at 180°c for 1¾ hours. Press and then leave the boulangère to cool, before cutting into batons.

continues over

Re-heat at the time of serving in a hot oven 180°c for 10 minutes.

Having soaked the sweetbreads overnight, remove any unwanted fat from them.

Rinse them well and then bring them up to the boil in a pan of water.

Refresh them in cold water and trim any visible sinews.

Place them into a clean pan with carrot, onion, bay leaf, white peppercorns and a pinch of salt. Top up with water and gently cook them for about 25 minutes.

Once cooked, remove them from the heat and leave them to cool in the cooking liquid. Once cold remove the sweetbreads and again check them over for sinew.

Break them into their natural pieces and, at the time of serving, dust them lightly with seasoned flour and pan fry them in the butter.

Firstly remove and throw away the green stalk and then cut the aubergine in half.

Score the flesh and lightly salt it and then leave it for 20 minutes before patting it dry.

Finely slice the garlic and tuck it into the score lines of the aubergine.

Sprinkle the two halves with the cumin seeds, drizzle with olive oil and bake it wrapped in tin foil at 180°c for 40 minutes.

Once cooked, scoop out the flesh and put it into a liquidizer.

Blend until smooth and then add the double cream. Pass the purée through a fine sieve to remove any seeds and season with salt and pepper.

Cooking and Dressing:

Season and seal the loins of lamb and then gently cook them either in the oven or on the top of the stove.

Ideally the lamb should be pink but not rare.

Once the degree of cooking you prefer has been reached, de-glaze the pan with the white wine, reduce and then add 100ml of lamb stock.

Bring back to the boil and reduce to a sauce consistency.

Neatly slice the loin into quite thick slices and arrange them on the plate with the purée and the potato.
Finish the dish with the sweetbreads and spring vegetables, I have used broad beans (shelled naturally!), asparagus, baby carrots and artichokes.

Lastly finish with a little of the sauce.

Chef's note:

The confit for the potato can easily be made the day before assembling the potato dish. The pressing can also take place overnight to make it really compact and easier to portion.

Best End of Lamb with Aubergine, Courgette, Toasted Cumin Seed Jus

Ingredients

4	6 bone best end of lamb, keep any bones or trimmings

Purée

2	aubergines
6	cloves garlic
2	sprigs thyme
50ml	double cream
1	pinch of cumin seeds
	olive oil
	lemon

Confit lamb

240g	middle neck of lamb fillet
	salt
	vegetable oil

Toasted cumin seed jus

25g	shallot
25g	carrot
1	pinch of cumin seeds, toasted in a dry pan and then ground with a pestle and mortar
175g	lamb trimmings
100ml	white wine
400ml	lamb or veal stock

Vegetables

2	aubergines
2	courgettes
200g	curly kale
200g	oyster mushrooms
24	sun dried tomato halves

Serves 8

I love the aroma of cumin, especially when the seeds are toasted. It isn't a spice that is in daily use but its wonderful flavour that really compliments lamb.

To make the purée, remove the stalks from the aubergines, cut in half lengthways, score and then salt them. After 20 minutes pat them dry on a cloth and brush with olive oil.

Peel and finely slice the garlic and, along with the cumin seeds and thyme, place on top of the aubergines. Cook in the oven covered with tin foil at 120°c for about 40 minutes until soft.

Once cooked, scoop out the flesh into a pan to evaporate any liquid. Add the cream and bring to the boil with a squeeze of lemon. Blend to a paste consistency and season. For a more refined purée, pass through a sieve.

Confit lamb from middle neck of lamb fillet. Salt the middle neck fillets for 45 minutes. Rinse off and cover with vegetable oil or rendered lamb fat and cook slowly in the oven at 120°c for a good couple of hours until tender. If the lamb starts to colour too much, cover with a little tin foil. Leave to cool and cut into 8 neat pieces.

Prepare a toasted cumin seed jus. Sauté the lamb trimmings with the shallot and carrots.

Deglaze with the white wine and reduce. Add the stock, bring to the boil and leave to cook gently.

Once this has reached a light sauce consistency add the cumin seeds and leave to infuse for 5 minutes, season and pass.

For the vegetables, cut the aubergines into 16 even, round slices. Salt for 20 minutes before patting them dry on a cloth and removing any excess salt, and either grill or lightly pan fry evenly in olive oil.

Keep a little of the oil for brushing later. Shape the courgettes with a sharp knife and cook them in a little water and butter. Pan fry the mushrooms and kale and re-heat the sundried tomatoes.

Serving:

Seal the lamb and cook in a pre-heated oven at 180°c for 15 minutes to be pink, turning a couple of times. Leave to rest while re-heating the confit.

Place a slice of aubergine in a ring and place the purée on top, then place a piece of the confit in the middle. Top with another slice of the aubergine and brush with a little aubergine oil.

Slice the lamb into cutlets, (three per person) and arrange the vegetables around.

Finally pour a little of the sauce onto the lamb.

Slow Roasted Shoulder of Lamb

Ingredients

Lamb shoulder

1	shoulder of lamb
3	cloves of garlic
2	sprigs of rosemary
	olive oil
	sea salt

Granny Dodson's hasty puddings

250g	self raising flour
2	pinch salt
4	pinch dried herbs
1	pinch dried mustard powder
100g	lard or margarine
50g	butter
	water to bind, approximately 45ml

Mint sauce

150ml	red wine vinegar
1	shallot, finely chopped
50g	sugar
15-20g	mint leaves, chopped

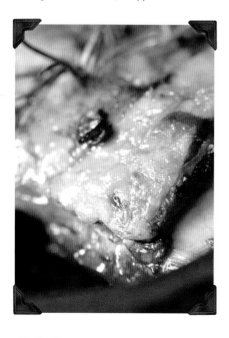

Serves 6/8

This meal just screams out Sunday lunch to me. It reminds me of a time when I would go home to my parents, have a swift couple of pints at 12 o'clock (on the dot, following the shipping forecast and the pips!) with my Dad at the Half Butt and be ready for lunch on the table at one o'clock sharp.

Of course it needs mint sauce and my grandmother's hasty puddings! The aroma of this lamb roasting takes me right back...

The method for the meat is so simple. Just make some indents in the skin of the lamb with a sharp knife and rub it with olive oil, slice the garlic and push it into the scores alternating with the rosemary, and season with sea salt.

Place it into a preheated oven 150°c and cook slowly for 2½ - 3 hours.

For Granny Dodson's hasty puddings, this seems quite a large recipe but these little savoury scones are so good you may want more than a couple.

Mix together all the dry ingredients and then rub in the lard and butter. Bind with the water to make a nice dough.

Roll it out approximately 2.5cm thick and with a cutter cut out 5.5cm circles.

Brush these with a little milk and sprinkle sea salt on top of them prior to cooking them.

Bake around the lamb joint or separately on a baking sheet for approximately 15 minutes at 185°c

To make the mint sauce, boil together the vinegar, sugar and shallot, leave to cool a little before adding the chopped mint and leave to infuse before serving.

Pan Roasted Veal Sweetbreads served with Sauce Diable

Ingredients

800g	veal sweetbread
1	onion cut in half
1	carrot cut lengthways
1	stick of celery
	a pinch of salt
	a bay leaf

Cos lettuce

2	cos lettuce
2	medium shallots, finely chopped
80g	butter
300ml	light veal or vegetable stock
	olive oil

Sauce diable

15ml	red wine vinegar
50ml	dry white wine
200ml	veal stock
1 pinch	crushed white peppercorns
25g	Chopped shallots
1	sprig tarragon
	salt and cayenne pepper

Serves 4

Offal can get a bad reputation for being strong tasting, which is quite unfair. So you may be surprised by the delicate flavour of sweetbreads.

Allow for 200g of veal sweetbread per person. This may seem a lot but there is a certain amount of trimming to be done. Two lobes of 400g each would be perfect. Soak the sweetbreads overnight to purge them of any blood, remove any unwanted fat and sinew from them. Rinse them well in running cold water and then place them into a pan of water and bring them up to the boil. Simmer for a minute and then refresh them. Once cold go over them again, removing any sinews.

In a fresh pan place the blanched sweetbreads with an onion cut in half, a carrot cut lengthways, a stick of celery, a pinch of salt and a bay leaf. Bring up to the boil and leave to simmer for 20 minutes. Leave to cool in the cooking liquor. Once cold, remove them and pat them dry.

Take 2 cos lettuces. Having removed a couple of the outer leaves, split the lettuces in half down the middle. Make a "v" cut in the stalk and remove it. In a tray, sweat the shallot without colour in a drizzle of olive oil and the butter. Add the lettuce, cut side down, and then the stock.

Cover with tin foil and braise in the oven at 160°c for 15 minutes, turning it once during cooking.

For the Sauce Diable, reduce together the red wine vinegar, dry white wine, crushed white peppercorns, chopped shallots, sprig of tarragon, salt and cayenne pepper. When almost dry add 200ml veal stock.

Remove the tarragon and reduce until the required consistency. Pass, season and add a pinch of cayenne pepper. If you prefer you can pass the sauce here to remove the shallot and peppercorns but I quite like the rustic look of the sauce with them left in.

Serving:

In a non-stick pan, melt 50g of butter with a drop of olive oil. Add the sweetbreads and cook them gently, basting all the time with the butter until it becomes a lovely golden brown.

When hot throughout, dress the lettuce onto the plate and slice the sweetbread onto this. Garnish with a brunoise of carrot and French beans and a potato fondant. Generously pour the sauce around and serve at once!

Chef's note:

If there is a bit of the lettuce cooking liquor left in the tray it can be passed and reduced and added to the sauce.

As an alternative after the cooking of the sweetbreads rather than pan roasting them whole, they can be sliced, breadcrumbed and shallow fried until golden. They are just as delicious!

Veal Chop with Sage & Parmesan Crust

Ingredients

4   veal chops

Sage crust

150g   white breadcrumbs
125g   softened butter
3g   sage, blanched and chopped
25g   parmesan cheese, finely grated
20g   Dijon mustard
1   egg yolk
10ml   double cream

Sage jus

25g   shallot
1   sprig of sage
50ml   white wine
200ml   veal stock

Potato fondants

3   potatoes, cut into 12
           fondants
50g   butter
250ml   water
1   sprig of thyme
           salt

Serves 4

Starting with the sage crust, in a food processor blend the breadcrumbs and the parmesan. Once mixed add the butter, mustard, cream, egg yolk and blend again. Finally add the chopped sage.

Turn out onto a piece of cling film, spread it out into a rectangular shape and cover with another piece of cling film and then with a rolling pin roll it flat to about 5mm thick.

Leave to set in the fridge before cutting out (still in the cling film) into four rectangles the size of the chops.

Next, the sage jus. Pick the four nicest sage leaves, blanch in boiling water for a few seconds, refresh and cut into julienne.

Slice the shallot and place in a pan with the wine and sage stalk and reduce until almost dry. Add the veal stock, bring back to the boil and leave to cook gently. Once this has reached a sauce consistency, pass and at the last minute add the julienne of sage and season.

These lovely potato fondants appear several times in the book, always cooked the same way but sometimes shaped differently. For this recipe the potatoes have been cut with a 3.5cm cutter.

In a suitable shallow pan place the potatoes, butter and thyme. Pour in the water, bring to the boil and leave to cook on the stove. As the water boils away the potatoes will start to colour in the butter.

The whole process should take about 35 minutes. If needed finish the potatoes off in the oven, they should be soft to eat but still holding. Remove the thyme before serving.

Cooking and serving:

Season and pan fry the veal chops leaving them slightly pink.

Once cooked pat the top of each one dry, carefully peel off the cling film from both sides of the crust and place a rectangle on top of each chop.

Finish cooking under the grill until golden.

Garnish with the fondants and, if in season, some peeled asparagus tips cooked in boiling water with a knob of butter and a pinch of salt. Lastly pour a little sage jus.

Chef's note:

This versatile crust can be used with any light meat or even with fish.

Grain mustard can be used instead of the Dijon mustard for a slightly different flavour.

Brisket of Beef with Dumplings

Ingredients

2	350g brisket mini joints
1	onion, cut into quarters
1	carrot, cut in half
1	leek, split
1	clove garlic
1	bay leaf
1	teaspoon white peppercorns

Garnish

8	baby carrots
8	new potatoes, pre-cooked and peeled
8	spring onions or baby leeks
12	baby onions

Dumplings

75g	self raising flour
10g	lard
10g	margarine
300ml	water
1	pinch of dried mustard powder
	salt and pepper

Horseradish cream

30g	creamed horseradish
50ml	bouillon
100ml	double cream

Serves 4

This is a winter's dish that is full of flavour but remarkably light to eat. The horseradish adds a real kick.

Season and seal the brisket in a hot pan and then add to a pan and cover with water, adding the onion, carrot, leek, garlic, bay leaf and white peppercorns.

Leave to simmer for 3-3½ hours until tender.

Don't let the liquid boil otherwise it will go cloudy.

Take time to skim any fat from the top. This will make a fantastic, flavoursome bouillon for poaching the dumplings and the vegetables.

Top up with water as necessary.

To make the dumplings, rub together the flour, mustard powder, salt, pepper, lard and margarine and then bind with the water.

Roll into 8 dumplings and poach them in a pan of the bouillon for about 20 minutes.

The horseradish cream is a must.

Boil the ingredients together and then pass through a fine sieve. Season and reserve.

If the cream starts to get too thick add a drop more of the bouillon to loosen.

Serving:

Cook the vegetables in a pan of the bouillon.

Portion and re-heat the potatoes. Slice the brisket and neatly arrange onto plates.

Pour some of the poaching liquor onto the dish then drizzle the horseradish cream onto the brisket.

Braised Beef Cheek in Red Wine

Ingredients

1.2kg	beef cheek
200ml	red wine
1	stick of celery
1	carrot
1	onion
	bay leaf and thyme
500ml	veal stock

Vegetables

12	new potatoes
200g	button onions
160g	Bbutton mushrooms
80g	bacon lardons, blanched
	chopped parsley

Serves 4

The classic Waterside Inn "daube de boeuf", we love this dish so much we chose it for our own winter wedding.

Trim the cheeks and cut into 12 equal sized pieces, put them to marinade with the red wine, the vegetables, the thyme and the bay leaf, leave overnight.

The following day lift out the cubes of meat and vegetables and pat them dry. Pour the wine into a sauce pan and bring it to the boil and give it a good skim before passing it through a fine sieve.

Season and seal the meat in a frying pan. When it is nicely coloured transfer the pieces into a saucepan. Also gently fry off the vegetables and then add them to the pan along with the herbs and the passed red wine. Bring it all to the boil and then add 500ml of veal stock, bring back to the boil and then reduce the heat to a very gentle simmer. Place a lid on top and leave it to cook for up to 5 hours. Be careful it doesn't become too dry and if necessary add a drop of water to the cooking.

Once cooked the meat should be soft to the touch but not falling apart. Remove the cubes of meat and place them onto a clean tray. Pass the cooking liquor, discarding the vegetables, and in a fresh pan leave it to reduce to a rich deep sauce consistency. Add the pieces of cheek back in keeping it all warm and prepare the garnish.

The best way that I've found to cook the new potatoes is to boil them in their skins. Once cooked they can be easily peeled with a sharp knife and then re-heated at the time of serving.

The button onions are best cooked in water with a pinch of salt, a pinch of sugar and a knob of butter. The button mushrooms are best sautèd in a little olive oil also with a good knob of butter. Half way through cooking add the lardons to the pan and colour them slightly.

Serving this dish is easy, make sure that the beef is nice and hot and that the sauce is gently boiling, add the onions to this (without their cooking liquor), and the mushrooms and lardons (which have been drained) re-heat the potatoes and roll them in butter and then in chopped parsley.

Chef's note:

Choose a red wine with a decent bit of body for the cooking, it's always worth checking the alcohol content!

Beef Fillet with Roasted Shallots & Sauté Potatoes, Green Peppercorn Sauce

Ingredients

4	160-180g fillet steaks
3	medium parsnips, approximately 375g
150ml	double cream
12	new potatoes
12	shallots
2	carrots
1	courgette
10g	soft green peppercorns
20ml	white wine
100ml	veal stock
100ml	double cream

Serves 4

Peel the parsnips and then use the peeler to slice one of them into long strips. Leave those strips to dry and then deep fry in hot oil. Leave to drain on absorbent paper, season and reserve until serving. Cut the remaining parsnips into 2cm dice, cover with water add a pinch of salt.

Place on a medium heat and cook until soft.

Drain well and return the parsnips to the the pan. Stir them round to evaporate the last of the liquid. Add the double cream and cook a little further. Blend in a liquidizer, season to taste, reserve and keep hot.

Next, peel the shallots and place in a pan. Cover with oil, add a bay leaf and a sprig of thyme.

Cook gently on the stove until a knife can be inserted into the shallot and it falls off the knife. Remove from the heat and reserve.

Cook the new potatoes in their skins in boiling salted water. Once cooked, refresh and peel while still slightly warm. Cut them in half lengthways and pan fry them golden brown in a little olive oil, a knob of butter and season.

To make the green peppercorn sauce, cook the soft green peppercorns in the white wine. When almost dry, add the veal stock, reduce by half and then add the cream, reduce again to the required consistency (the sauce should coat the back of a spoon).

Season with a little salt and a drop of Tabasco if you are feeling brave.

Serving:

Cook the steaks to your preference in a lightly oiled hot pan and add the shallots to the same pan. In boiling water cook some carrot ribbons and courgette balls and divide the purée between the four plates.

Place the potatoes on the plate with the steak on top. Garnish with the carrot ribbons and courgettes. Pour the sauce over the steaks and top with the the deep-fried parsnip crisps.

Beef Wellington, Potato Gratin & Red Wine Jus

Ingredients

1kg	beef fillet, cut from the centre of the fillet
1kg	puff pastry
	salt and pepper

Mushroom duxelle

800g	button mushrooms, chopped
1	shallot, finely chopped
150ml	double cream

Pancakes (makes 6)

100g	flour
275ml	milk
1	egg
1	pinch dried herbs
	salt and pepper

Red wine jus

400ml	red wine
1	sprig of thyme
100g	shallot, sliced
400ml	veal stock

Potato gratin

4	potatoes, 350g each
3	cloves garlic
400ml	double cream
5g	salt

Serves 8

Prepare the mushroom duxelle by sweating the finely chopped shallot in a little oil, adding the chopped mushrooms and cooking until dry. Finally add the cream and cook until thick, season and leave to cool before using.

With a hand blender or whisk, mix together all of the pancake ingredients and fry the pancakes thinly and without too much colour in a non-stick pan.

Season and seal the beef in a hot pan and give it 5minutes in a hot oven (200°c). Leave the beef in longer, should you require it to be more well-cooked.

Cool on a wire rack and pat dry with absorbent paper.

Roll out the pastry to an oblong to generously fit the fillet and line it with the pancakes.

Try not to overlap the pancakes as they are only there to make a seal between the mushroom and the pastry.

Spread the duxelles onto the fillet and place it on top of the pancake.

Bring up the two sides of pastry to enclose the fillet, trimming any excess. Seal the seam and the ends well with egg wash and then egg wash the whole piece.
With the point of a small knife make two small holes for any steam to escape during cooking.

Any pastry trimmings can be used for decoration.

Leave to rest in a cool place before cooking. Place into a pre-heated oven at 180°c for approximately 35-40 minutes.

The pastry should be golden and the beef fillet hot inside.

For the jus, make a reduction of the wine, thyme and shallot.

Once almost dry, add the stock and reduce to an almost syrupy consistency. Season and pass before using.

Make the potato gratin by rubbing a suitable baking dish with one of the garlic cloves. Add that and the remaining garlic to the cream and bring to the boil.

Leave to simmer for a minute or two. Peel and thinly slice the potatoes. Season and place neatly into the dish.

Pass the garlic cream onto them and bake in a pre-heated oven at 160°c for approximately 1½ hours.

Chef's note:

Whilst it may be tempting to use a food processor to chop the mushrooms, they will be much less watery if chopped with a knife.

This is ...

GAME

Breasts of Wood Pigeon with Curried Brussels Sprout Purée and Stuffing

Ingredients

4	wood pigeon
1	medium sized potato
100ml	chicken stock
100ml	veal stock
1	carrot
1	shallot
100g	wild mushrooms
	thyme

Purée

250g	sprouts
50g	butter
5g	mild curry powder
225ml	double cream
	salt

Stuffing

275g	sausage meat
5g	sage, chopped
½	onion, finely chopped
½	zest from ½ an orange
½	zest from ½ a lemon
65g	peeled chopped chestnuts
10ml	brandy
	salt and pepper

Serves 4

This is a Masons Arms classic that makes the most of delicious, flavoursome game with a fantastic sauce and stuffing.

The purée is also delicious and I have converted many a non-lover of sprouts with this recipe.

Cook the sprouts thoroughly in boiling salted water. Drain them and in the same pan, cook them in the butter.

When sizzling, add the curry powder and cook for a good minute. Add the cream and bring back to the boil. Blend in a liquidiser until smooth then correct the seasoning.

The stuffing is made by sweating the onions, adding the zests and brandy. Flame, reduce the liquid, then add the sage.

Chop the chestnuts and add to the pan. Leave to cool and when cold add the sausage meat. Mix well and season.

Lay out a square of cling film, place the stuffing mixture on top and roll into a sausage shape about 2 inches round. Poach in simmering water for 10-15 minutes.

Remove the legs and breasts from the pigeon. Remove the skin and discard. Keep the breasts until needed.

In a pan, with a little oil, cook and colour the pigeon legs along with the diced carrot, diced shallot and a sprig of thyme. De-glaze with white wine and leave to reduce.

Cover with the two stocks and cook gently for half an hour, skimming regularly. Season, pass and reduce to the required sauce consistency.

Once cool, unwrap the stuffing and cut into four equal circular slices. Cut the potatoes with the help of a mandolin into criss-cross slices. Wash and drain them before deep frying them in hot oil until golden.

Serving:

Lightly pan fry the pigeon breasts with the slices of stuffing and the mushrooms, ideally the pigeon should be served pink but not too rare. Re-heat and place some purée onto the plate. Dress the pigeon on top of the stuffing. Pour a little of the sauce around and garnish with the mushrooms and deep fried potatoes.

Roasted Partridge with Stuffed Cabbage & Tarragon Jus

Ingredients

6	partridge
1	carrot
1	stick of celery
2	shallots
1tsp	tomato purée
	sprouts
	parsnips
	sprigs of tarragon
150ml	chicken stock
150ml	veal stock

Cabbage

1	600g savoy cabbage
1	small onion finely sliced
1	clove garlic, crushed
100g	butter
100ml	white wine
	freshly ground pepper

Serves 6

As a customer once said to me, "that's the biggest Brussels sprout I have ever seen!"

Prepare the partridges for roasting by removing the wing tips and neck. If necessary singe the last few feathers from the birds.

Make a stock from the wing tips and necks with the carrot, celery, shallots and the tomato purée as well as a good few sprigs of tarragon. Cover with half and half chicken and veal stock.

Remove the very outer leaves of the cabbage and then carefully unfurl the next six leaves and keep them to one side for filling.

Cut the remaining cabbage into quarters, core and finely shred. Melt the butter in a suitable pan, add the onion and garlic, cook a little then add the cabbage and the white wine and cook for about 15 minutes until tender but still keeping its colour. Season with salt and pepper and keep until needed.

Blanch the 6 remaining leaves in boiling salted water until the stem is soft and then refresh in iced water. Drain and leave to dry on a cloth. Tear 6 squares of cling film and lay the leaves on them.

Divide the cabbage between them and then gather up each leaf into a ball shape and tie with the remaining cling film into a ball ready for re-heating.

Season the partridges and then seal in a hot pan with a little oil ensuring the leg area is browned on both sides.

Blanch the sprouts and parsnips for a couple of minutes and place around the birds to roast. Cook the partridges on their backs for approximately 15 minutes in a pre-heated oven at 180-200°C. Once cooked, de-glaze the pan with white wine and add to the stock.

After resting the birds remove the breasts and legs. Quickly chop and add the carcass to the stock and back bring to the boil.

Serving:

Pass and reduce the stock but still keep it at a fairly light sauce consistency. Gently remove any fat from the top of the sauce.

Pass through a fine sieve on to some diced tarragon and adjust the seasoning.
Drop the stuffed cabbage leaves into a pan of simmering water.

Sauté some wild mushrooms with a little chopped shallot.

Arrange the partridge in the middle of the plate, circled by the vegetables and gently pour the sauce over the birds.

Chef's note:

If you like add a few smoked bacon lardons to the cabbage. I also love bread sauce and would recommend it with this partridge.

Breast of Pheasant with Choucroute & Sausage

Ingredients

2	hen pheasants

Choucroute

100g	onion
500g	choucroute cabbage
200g	Morteau
8	juniper berries
1	bay leaf
150ml	white wine

Pheasant mousse sausage

160g	thigh meat
1	egg white
100ml	double cream
	salt

Serves 4

As everyone in Devon seems to have a freezer full of them, we don't often put pheasant on the menu at the Masons Arms. However, this is a great recipe that utilises the whole bird. Dry pheasant is what gives it a bad name so be brave and don't overcook it.

Remove the wishbones and portion the pheasants into breasts and legs. Cut the legs in two, separating the thighs from the drumsticks. The breasts are for the main part of the dish, the thighs for the mousse sausage and the drumsticks for the stock.

For the choucroute, finely slice the onion and sweat without colour in a little olive oil. Rinse the cabbage in a colander and then add it to the onion, with the juniper berries and bay leaf. Pour in the white wine and bury the Morteau (as a whole piece) in the cabbage, cover and cook for at least an hour.

To make pheasant mousse sausage, skin and trim any fat from the thighs, and remove the thigh bone. Dice the meat and blend to a paste in a food processor with the egg white and a pinch of salt.

Rub it through a drum sieve. It is pretty hard work but the only way to get it smooth. Set the paste in a bowl on ice and gradually beat in the double cream in about 20ml measures. Once incorporated, season, divide into 8 and then wrap individually in cling film. Roll into sausage shapes, tying both ends. Place into water just below simmering and poach for 10 minutes, transfer to cold water and cool. Once cold unwrap them and then coat in flour, egg wash and breadcrumb.

To serve, gently pan fry them in a little oil with a good knob of butter.

Serving:

In a hot pan pour a little oil, place the pheasant breasts in skin side down and colour them. Add a good knob of butter, and cook for 10-12 minutes (depending on size) in a preheated oven at 180°c, basting them often.

Dress the sliced pheasant breast with the sliced Morteau and the sausage on a generous bed of choucroute with a little liquor around and some simple buttered new potatoes with snipped parsley.

Chef's note:

I would use the hen pheasant in preference, it is slightly smaller and often more tender.

Morteau is a raw juniper and conifer smoked sausage from the Jura. It is one of my absolute favourites and there really is no substitute. Bearing in mind that it is raw you may wish to blanch it in simmering water for 20 minutes before adding it to the choucroute.

The sausage mousse recipe will make more than you need but poach them all off and why not try a couple for breakfast the next day with a fried egg, pheasant of course.

Wild Duck with Fig & Cranberries

Ingredients

2	wild ducks
4	figs
4	Jerusalem artichokes

Sauce

75g	sugar
100ml	red wine vinegar
1	shallot, diced
1	carrot, diced
200ml	veal stock
200ml	chicken stock

Pearl barley risotto

120g	pearl barley, soaked overnight
½	onion, finely chopped
50ml	white wine
200ml	chicken or vegetable stock
75ml	double cream
30g	Parmesan, finely grated olive oil

Cranberries

60g	cranberries
200ml	port
1 tbsp	sugar
1	strip of orange peel

Serves 4

This vinegary sweet sauce cuts through the richness of the duck beautifully.

Remove the wishbones and take off the two breasts from each duck, then remove the legs. Chop up the carcass and keep it for the sauce.

For the sauce, heat a little olive oil in a pan and add the chopped carcass, shallot and carrot. Once coloured, add the sugar and cook for a minute or two. De-glaze with the red wine vinegar and bring back to the boil.

Add the veal stock and chicken stock and leave to cook gently. After an hour pass the sauce through a fine sieve and reduce to a sauce consistency.

To make the pearl barley risotto, heat the oil in a pan and sweat the onion so it is soft but not coloured. Rinse and add the pearl barley to the pan and stir with a spatula.

Add the white wine and bring to the boil for a minute. Add the stock and bring back to the boil. Stir often until the barley is tender and the stock is reduced, which should take about 20 minutes.

Add the cream and re-boil. Finally add the grated Parmesan. Season if necessary, bearing in mind the saltiness of the cheese.

To prepare the cranberries, boil the port with the sugar and the orange peel. Add the cranberries and re-boil. Cover the pan with cling film and leave to cool.

Peel, finely slice, wash and dry a couple of Jerusalem artichokes. At the last minute deep fry them in very hot oil to make crisps. Drain them on kitchen paper and sprinkle with salt.

Top and tail the figs and then with a sharp knife make four cuts across the top giving 8 segments. Be careful to only cut the fig two thirds of the way down. Dust with icing sugar and then colour under the grill. As the fig cooks the segments should open up.

Cooking and serving:

In a hot pan brushed with oil, season and cook the duck breasts and legs, starting with the skin-side down. Once the breast is cooked pink, remove it from the pan to rest but give the legs an extra five minutes

Once rested, carve the duck and arrange onto the plates with the leg and fig. Place the pearl barley onto the plates and drop the cranberries into the sauce. Cook and arrange 120g of French beans and pour a little of the sauce around. Finally add the deep-fried Jerusalem artichokes.

Chef's note:

If the Jerusalem artichokes are to be peeled in advance place them in water with a squeeze of lemon to stop them discolouring.

Loin of Venison with Poached Pear & Blue Cheese Gratin

Ingredients

600g	venison loin from the saddle

Venison sauce

	venison bones and trimmings
2	carrots, chopped
1	onion, chopped
1	stick of celery, chopped
1	tbsp tomato purée
	water, to cover
2	tbsp pear poaching liquid

Blue cheese gratin

4	medium potatoes, peeled
75ml	milk
140ml	double cream
3	cloves of garlic
200g	blue cheese, we use Gorgonzola

Poached pears

2	pears , peeled, halved, cored
200ml	red wine
100g	sugar
1	cinnamon stick

Serves 4

Remove 600g venison loin from the saddle (trimmed, portioned into 4 x 150g pieces – retaining any bones and trimmings for the sauce)

Prepare the sauce ahead by preheating the oven to 180°c and roasting the bones and trimmings for 45 minutes until golden brown.

In a separate pan lightly fry off the vegetables and once coloured add the tomato purée, sweat again and then cover with water.

Leave the stock to cook slowly for 6-8 hours. Once cooked, pass through a fine sieve and reduce until a good consistency is achieved.

Just before serving, reduce a couple of spoonfuls of the pear poaching liquid and add to the sauce to give a little depth and sweetness.

For the blue cheese gratin, preheat the oven to 150°c. Boil together the milk, cream, garlic and cheese.

Slice the potatoes and place evenly in a suitable dish, pass the liquid onto the slices. Cover the top of the dish with greaseproof paper and bake in the oven for 1-1½ hours. Halfway through cooking, press down on the potatoes to ensure the gratin is compact, once cooked the potato should have a good colour and be soft all the way through.

Now poach the pears in the red wine with the sugar and the cinnamon stick until just cooked. Leave them to cool in the liquid.

To serve:

Cook the venison in a pan until pink and leave it to rest before slicing. Cook the vegetables as desired, we have used salsify, cavolo nero and baby carrots. Arrange the meat on the plate with the vegetables and add a good piece of the gratin. Slice and fan the pear before finally pouring a little of the sauce around the dish.

Chef's note:

Venison needn't be a strong meat. Take it off the bone and lightly cover it in olive oil. Place it in a container with a few juniper berries and a bay leaf and store in the fridge for up to 5 days.

Fillet of Hare with Flaked Braised Leg

Ingredients

1	hare
20ml	olive oil
2	juniper berries, crushed
1	bay leaf
1	onion, chopped
1	carrot, chopped
2	sticks of celery, chopped
2	cloves of garlic, halved
1	dessert spoon tomato purée
200ml	red wine
120ml	double cream
2	large potatoes shaped into 4 fondants
6	large brussels sprouts broken down into leaves
40g	wild mushrooms
12	peeled chestnuts
1	punnet redcurrants
	redcurrant jelly

Stock

1	onion, chopped
1	carrot, chopped
2	sticks of celery, chopped
1	dessert spoon tomato purée

Serves 4

Another one of my favourites, hare needn't be strong, just don't leave it hanging around too long.

Begin by jointing the hare. Remove the shoulders and back legs, then gently take off the two fillets from the back of the hare and trim away all the sinew.

Place the fillets into a suitable container and cover with the olive oil and add the crushed juniper berries and a bay leaf.

Marinate the legs in the red wine with the onion, celery, carrot and garlic. Refrigerate both the legs and fillets and leave for 24 hours.

To make the stock, chop the carcass and the shoulders and lightly roast in the oven. In a suitable pan colour the onion, carrot, celery with the tomato purée, add the hare bones, cover with water and leave to cook for at least 4 hours, pass and then reduce.

Remove the legs from the marinade and pass the liquid into a pan (keep the vegetables back for braising).

Bring to the boil and remove any impurities from the top by skimming the surface, then pass and reserve. Pat the legs dry, season and seal in a pan with the vegetables, de-glaze with the passed red wine marinade, bring back to the boil and reduce by a third before covering with the stock.

Leave to cook in a covered pan until the meat is soft, this will take 2-3 hours depending on the size of the legs.

Once cooked, leave the legs to cool and then flake off the meat but be very careful not to include any bone.

Pass the cooking liquor and simmer to reduce by a half.

Serving:

Place the leg meat into a suitable pan, moisten with some of the reduced stock and bring to the boil.

Bind the meat with the double cream, season and reserve.

Reduce the remaining stock to a sauce consistency - at this point a little redcurrant jelly can be added to give a hint of sweetness.

Take the fillets from the oil, season and gently pan fry so that they remain pink.

Flash fry some sprout leaves and wild mushrooms so they still have some texture.

Divide the leg meat between 4 plates and slice the fillets, allowing half a fillet per person, garnish with the sprout leaves, chestnuts, mushrooms and a good hearty potato such as a potato fondant.

Pass and then pour the finished sauce around the dish and garnish with a few redcurrants to give a little bite and a touch of colour.

Roasted Grouse with Bread Sauce

Ingredients

4	grouse

Farce au gratin

60g	pork fat (cut into small dice)
150g	livers, from the grouse and topped up with chicken livers
40g	butter, soft but not melted
30ml	port
1	sprig of thyme
½	bay leaf
	brandy
	salt

Jus

	white wine
100ml	chicken stock
100ml	veal stock

Bread sauce

50g	butter
1	medium sized onion, 150g
500ml	milk
1	bay leaf
8	cloves
5	slices white bread, crusts off and cubed
	salt

Serves 4

Chefs love the start of the game season because the magnificent grouse is the gateway to all of the autumn flavours. We often served grouse on the glorious 12th at The Waterside Inn.

As Diego, the restaurant manager, used to say: "Smell the grouse... smell the holiday coming!"

In those days we worked from February until Boxing Day so January was always the month to look forward to.

I remember the first time I saw the grouse being served at The Waterside. Chef Roux was on the pass and the commis chef on the veg section was cooking the sprouts gently in a frying pan.

They were dark golden, almost too dark for most, and very buttery. I thought they were over cooked and the young chef was going to get a proper telling off.

When it came to serving them Michel tasted one and proclaimed "excellent sprouts my lad!". And from that day on I have cooked them the same... I just love sprouts his way.

Make a farce au gratin. This beautiful farce is a classical accompaniment to grouse.

The livers can be soaked in milk overnight making them less strong. Adding chicken livers to the grouse livers also makes the farce milder. In a non-stick pan cook down the pork fat gently until there is a melted covering of the oil. Into this place the livers, the thyme and bay leaf.

Turn up the heat and cook the livers until pink.

Flambé with a drop of brandy and then de-glaze with the port.

Reduce a little and then pass the contents of the pan through a fine sieve into a bowl.

Stir in the softened butter and season with a pinch of salt. Leave it to set in a cool place and then spread it onto fried bread croûtons to be reheated at the time of serving.

For the bread sauce, cut the onion in half through the core.

Finely chop one half and sweat without colour in the butter in a suitable saucepan.

Pour on the milk and bring to the boil. Leave it on a very low heat. Stud the other half of the onion with the bay leaf and cloves and add to the milk.

Cook very gently for 20 minutes. Once infused, add a pinch of salt and the cubed bread.

Cook until thickened. Just prior to serving give the sauce a quick boil, being careful that it doesn't catch.

If you prefer a smooth bread sauce whisk it a little.

continues over

In a hot pan seal the bird all round and then cook it in a pre-heated oven at 180°c for 15-20 minutes, giving it 5 minutes on each leg and at least 5 minutes on its back.

Leave to rest before serving. If you are worried about it getting cold, cover it loosely with tin foil.

De-glaze the pan with a drop of white wine, reduce and then add the stocks, reduce to a good consistency but not too thick.

Put the croûton into the oven to re-heat and if necessary finish under the grill to colour.

We have served our grouse with a traditional potato basket filled with "pommes parisiennes", Brussels sprouts, leaf spinach and deep fried parsley.

Chef's note:

The grouse should be checked over for feathers and shot.

It's always best to remove the wishbone before cooking, especially if you are eating it on the bone, which is always preferred.

Tying a rasher of bacon to the breast is a lovely idea and also gives a great taste.

For the smaller appetite a grouse between two would suffice, though personally I would prefer a whole one.

Traditional Roasted Woodcock served on a Croûton

Ingredients

1	woodcock
1	king oyster mushroom, eryngii
2	potatoes
1	carrot
2	sprouts
1	crouton
	chicken stock
	veal stock

Serves 1

This is not so much a recipe but more of a method for use if you are lucky enough to have a woodcock.

Allow 1 bird per person

For me woodcock is the king of game birds. I love its oily texture. It's odd to think that in the depths of our winter, woodcock have flown here from Scandinavia to avoid colder weather. They generally migrate south on a full moon so as the weather gets colder keen guns look forward to a woodcock moon. Some consider this to be coincidence but it does seem to ring true. Here in Devon we don't see too many until December.

I have seen woodcock prepared in more modern ways but I prefer to serve it simply roasted with its head on, but eyes removed with the tip of a knife, and the entrails still inside. Only the gizzard needs to be discarded after cooking as that will still have undigested food within.

Pluck and singe over an open flame to remove the last few feathers from the bird.

Neatly pierce the beak through the thighs to truss it. Season the bird and in a suitable pan pour in a little oil and seal the bird with a good knob of butter. Roast in a pre-heated oven at 180°c for approximately 10 minutes basting it every 2-3 minutes - this will leave the bird cooked pink.

Rest and wrap it loosely in tin foil. De-glaze the pan with a little white wine and then add 50-50 chicken stock and veal stock. Leave to reduce slightly.

Prepare one croûton per person approximately the same size as the bird. It can either be toasted or pan fried.

After a couple of minutes of resting, remove the entrails with a teaspoon, look for the gizzard and discard it (the gizzard is hard to the touch and oval in shape). Chop the entrails with a cook's knife, moisten with a splash of brandy and port and for extra richness add a cube of foie gras. Season with salt and a couple of turns of the peppermill. Spread the mixture onto the croûton and place it back into the oven or under a grill for a couple of minutes until it is hot.

Remove the head at the top of the neck and by cutting down the beak split the head in half. The brain will then be revealed – this delicacy should be eaten first. Remove the wishbone and gently cut down each side of the breast bone, which will making eating easier and will also enable you to check the cooking.

Add the wishbone and the neck to the sauce. Stud the bird with the beak and place it onto the croûton, pass the sauce. Season and serve immediately.

As the woodcock is so rich keep the garnish simple. I have used a slice of grilled king oyster mushroom (eryngii) a couple of roast potatoes, some carrot balls and some stir fried sprout leaves.

Chef's note:

Woodcock is a beautiful bird, uncommon and difficult to shoot, so should be given the respect it deserves.

This is ...

DESSERTS

Mixed Berry Crème Brûlée

Ingredients

6	egg yolks
60g	sugar
250ml	double cream.
	mixed berries to garnish the crème brûlée
	demerara sugar for glazing

Serves 6

The beauty of this dish lies in its simplicity but, as with many simple dishes, to achieve a great result it must be cooked to perfection.

Whisk together the egg yolks and the sugar. Boil the cream and pour it onto the yolks, pass and reserve.

Once cooled, this mixture can be refrigerated until needed.

Place the berries into the dishes allowing four blueberries, a couple of raspberries cut in half and a strawberry cut into six or eight, per portion. Top up the dishes with the crème brûlée mixture.

Prepare a bain-marie by placing a paper towel into a deep oven tray and place the crème brûlées into the tray. Pour a little water around them but not so much as to run into them.

This method will prevent the mixture boiling during cooking, which would give a "split" appearance to the finished dish.

Bake the brûlées in a low oven, pre-heated to 130°c.

Depending on the oven and on the serving dishes chosen, check the cooking after 20 minutes.

Bear in mind that they could take up to 30 minutes to cook if you choose a deeper style serving dish.

The brûlées should appear just-set when the dish is gently shaken.

Once cooked, leave them to cool and then at serving time sprinkle the tops with demerara sugar and carefully glaze them with a blowtorch.

Chef's note:

Now you have a basic Crème Brûlée recipe why not experiment with different flavours?

Rhubarb & Sweet Wine Trifle

Sponge

50g	butter
50g	sugar
50g	flour
¼	pinch of baking powder
1	drop of vanilla essence
1	egg
	raspberry jam

Crème Anglaise

200ml	double cream
100ml	milk
70g	sugar
½	vanilla pod, split
4	yolks

Jelly

300ml	sweet wine
150g	sugar
1 tsp	grenadine
½	vanilla pod
3	leaves gelatine, pre-soaked
250g	rhubarb in small dice

Serves 4

From the beginning, another early dessert. If no rhubarb is available try it with mixed berries.

Cream together the butter and sugar, add the egg and then the sieved flour and baking powder.

Spoon into a buttered and lined baking tray with sides, approx 8 x 20 cm. If necessary use folded greaseproof paper as an edge.

Bake for 7-10 minutes at 180°c, leave to cool on a wire rack.

Cut the sponge horizontally through the middle and sandwich the sponge with raspberry jam and cut into 1.5cm cubes.

For the crème Anglaise, boil together the cream, milk, 50g of the sugar and the vanilla pod.

Beat together the yolks with the remaining sugar.

Once boiling pour the milk and cream onto the yolks, mix well and return to the pan.

Cook until the sauce coats the back of a spoon.

Pass the sauce through a fine sieve and keep to one side until needed.

Make a jelly by bringing to the boil the wine, sugar, grenadine and the vanilla, and pass.

Add the rhubarb and cook until soft, finally add the disolved gelatine.

In a suitable glass place 4 cubes of the sponge and cover with the rhubarb jelly leaving enough room for the Anglaise and let it set for at least an hour.

At the time of serving pour on the crème Anglaise, decorate with some grated milk chocolate or toasted almonds and serve on a side plate with sablé biscuits.

Chocolate & Caramelised Hazelnut Mousse

Ingredients

125ml	double cream
50g	milk chocolate
125g	gianduja, chocolate and hazelnut paste
2	yolks
250ml	whipped double cream
40g	blanched hazelnuts
60g	sugar

Butterscotch sauce

80g	soft light brow 25g sieved flour

Serves 4-6

Definitely one of my top 10 desserts, I think this one started life at The Waterside Inn.

The praline

Bake the hazelnuts in a warm oven, 160°c, on a dry tray for about 10 minutes. Cook a light caramel with the sugar and a drop of water and then add the hazelnuts, making sure they are coated in the caramel.

Turn out and leave to cool on baking mat and chop a little with a large knife or pulse briefly in a blender.

The mousse

Boil the double cream and pour onto the gianduja and milk chocolate, ensuring it is completely melted. Add the egg yolks and whisk together well.

Cool and then fold in the lightly whipped cream and the hazelnut praline. Set in moulds or in a suitable dish.

Butterscotch sauce

In a suitable pan, cook together the sugar and butter and then add the cream. Re-boil and pass through a fine sieve, leave to cool before serving.

Brandy snap biscuit

Mix together the butter, sugar and golden syrup and then add the flour, beat it until smooth and then leave it in the fridge to firm up before rolling slightly flattened balls about an inch round, space them well on a baking mat and cook in a pre-heated oven at 180°c for 3 to 4 minutes. Leave to cool before removing them.

Serving

Turn out the mousses and surround them with the butterscotch sauce, top with the brandy snap biscuit and if you wish a swirl of crème anglaise.

Chef's note:

You may need to seek out a specialist supplier for the gianduja but it will be well worth it!

Mango Parfait with Coconut Sorbet

Ingredients

Parfait

6	egg yolks
375ml	double cream
100g	caster sugar
250ml	mango purée

Mango coulis

100g	mango purée
15g	caster sugar

Diced tropical fruit

50ml	water
50g	caster sugar
1	kiwi fruit
1	papaya
½	mango
8	strawberries

Coconut biscuits

35g	melted butter
50g	icing sugar
55g	egg whites
15g	flour
50g	desiccated coconut

Coconut sorbet

240ml	water
150g	sugar
60g	glucose
400ml	coconut milk

Serves 8

This is such a beautiful summer dessert, with the sweetness of the mango and creaminess of the sorbet balance one another perfectly. The diced tropical fruits gives it an exotic edge while the coconut biscuit spiral adds both a presentational flourish and texture.

To make the parfait, whip the cream until soft peaks form and then return to the fridge. Using a whisk attachment beat the egg yolks on a high speed with one tablespoon of warm water until they double in size.

Cook the sugar with just enough water to cover it to soft ball (116°c) and slowly pour down the edge of the mixing bowl to combine with the yolks while mixing.

Once the mix has cooled, add the mango purée until combined. Lastly fold in the cream, place in 7cm moulds and set in the freezer for a minimum of 4 hours.

For the coulis, bring ingredients to the boil, pass and reserve until needed.

For the diced fruit, bring the water and sugar to the boil, leave to cool and then add the carefully diced fruit.

To make the coconut biscuits, mix together the sugar, flour and coconut, then add the butter and egg whites. Mix well and then leave in the fridge to become firm.

With an oblong template spread the mix thinly onto a baking sheet and cook in a pre-heated oven at 180°c for 4-5 minutes until golden. While they are still warm curl them around a sharpening steel to give a spiral shape.

Make a sorbet syrup by boiling together the water, sugar and glucose. Leave it to go cold and then mix it with the coconut milk. Pass it through a fine sieve and churn in an ice cream machine.

Serving:

Serve each parfait glazed with a little of the mango coulis and a quenelle of the coconut sorbet. Garnish with the tropical fruit, a little of the coulis and reduction of balsamic vinegar. To really top the dessert off carefully place a coconut biscuit spiral on top of the sorbet.

Chef's note:

The sorbet recipe will make more than is needed but will be a great back up to have in the freezer.

Cream Cheese Panna Cotta with Caramelised Pineapple

Ingredients

Panna cotta

225g	marscapone or Philadelphia cheese
75g	caster sugar
100ml	double cream
2	vanilla pods, split
1½	leaves of dissolved gelatine leaves
300ml	lightly whipped cream

Pineapple garnish

1	small pineapple
50g	butter
50g	soft dark brown sugar
1	teaspoon soft green peppercorns
25ml	dark rum
50ml	water

Serves 6

This isn't a traditional panna cotta: the addition of cream cheese means less gelatine.

The spicy pineapple gives it a real edge, combining sweet, sharp and a hint of heat.

It's a truly vibrant dish that makes for delicious eating.

Boil together ingredients for the panna cotta – marscapone or Philadelphia cheese, caster sugar, double cream and vanilla pods (split).

Then add 1½ dissolved gelatine leaves, pass and leave to cool.

Finally, fold in 300ml of lightly whipped cream.
Pour into moulds and leave to set in the fridge.

Peel and then slice a pineapple into 6 length wise pieces, remove the core.

Melt together the butter and soft dark brown sugar, add the pineapple and caramelise a little.

Add the rum, water and the soft green peppercorns and gently cook until soft.

At the time of serving, cut the pineapple into small pieces and re-heat them.

Neatly arrange them around the panna cotta with a few of the peppercorns and pour a little of the syrup around.

Chef's note:

This rich dessert may benefit from a little crunch. Try our cigarette biscuit recipe.

Toffee & Banana Mille-Feuille

Ingredients

Croquant biscuit

80g	sieved icing sugar
30g	flour
2 tbs	milk
20g	melted butter
1	large pinch mixed spice

Banana mousse

250g	banana purée or equivalent of sieved banana
2	sheets of leaf gelatine, soaked in cold water
140ml	lightly whipped double cream
40g	sugar
1 tsp	glucose
1	egg white, already started beating and becoming frothy

Toffee

20g	butter
20g	soft dark brown sugar
160g	condensed milk
20ml	double cream

Banana Anglaise

60g	banana purée
120ml	double cream
60ml	milk
3	egg yolks
1	pinch of sugar

Pecan praline cream

60g	sugar
40g	pecan nuts
140ml	double cream
10g	icing sugar

Serves 6

Quite a lot of work goes into this dish but it's worth it. After all, who can resist the combination of toffee and bananas?

Roll out 300g of puff pastry into a rectangle measuring 40cm x 26cm and cook between 2 baking sheets in a pre-heated oven at 180°c until golden (15- 20 minutes).

Once cold cut it into rectangles measuring 10.5cm x 4.5cm.

For the croquant biscuit, mix together all of the ingredients.

Transfer into a suitable container and leave in the fridge to firm up. Then with a template, spread the mixture onto a baking mat into rectangles the same size as the puff pastry and bake at 180°c for 4-5 minutes until golden.

Next, for the banana mousse, make an Italian meringue, cook together the sugar and glucose with just enough water to cover it to 116°c (soft ball) then pour onto the egg white and whisk until cool.

Take 40g of the banana purée, bring it to the boil, add the gelatine, mix together and add to the remaining puree.

Fold this into the cream, followed by the Italian meringue.

Pour into a fairly shallow tray (18cm x 24cm) lined with cling film and leave it to set. Leave overnight and then cut into rectangles 10.5cm x 4.5cm and wrap them individually in baking parchment.

To make toffee, melt the butter and sugar in a heavy bottomed pan and then add the condensed milk.

Bring it to the boil and finally add the double cream and re-boil.

Leave it to cook for a couple of minutes being careful that it doesn't catch or burn on the bottom.

Pass through a fine sieve and place it into a piping bag and refrigerate until cold. Leave it to come round to room temperature before dressing.

For banana Anglaise, whisk together the yolks and sugar. In a separate pan bring to the boil the purée, cream and milk and pour it onto the egg yolks.

Return it to the pan and cook until the mixture coats the back of a spoon, being careful not let it boil.

Pass and leave to cool, covering with cling film and touching the sauce to prevent a skin forming.

continues over

Pecan praline cream is made by cooking a caramel with the sugar and a drop of water and then adding the pecan nuts, making sure they are coated in the caramel.

Turn out and leave to cool on baking mat. Once cold place into a food processor, cover your ears and crush it down!

Whisk the cream so that it is stiff and then add the sugar and finally fold in the praline.

To assemble:

Take the rectangles of puff pastry and carefully place the banana mousse on top followed by another piece of the puff pastry.

Pipe alternate "buttons" of the toffee and praline cream and then top with the croquant biscuit.

Finish with the banana anglaise and serve with a rich ice cream, such as our clotted cream ice cream.

Chef's note:

This wonderful dessert does have quite a few elements but to spread the workload a few of them, such as the banana mousse and croquant biscuit, can be made the day before.

To make the template for the biscuit, carefully cut a rectangle out of the top of an ice cream container with a craft knife.

Pineapple, Shortbread & Lemon Cream

Ingredients

Shortbread biscuit

40g	ground almonds
325g	flour
200g	butter
130g	icing sugar
2	eggs
	grated zest of lemon
	pinch of salt

Lemon cream

75g	lemon juice & zest of 2 lemons
150g	sugar
100g	butter
3	eggs

Pineapple

1	large sweet pineapple
20g	caster sugar
20ml	water
1	drop of good quality vanilla essence
50g	butter
100g	light soft brown sugar

Serves 6

This is one of the earliest Masons desserts, vintage 2005. It's remained popular ever since. The layer of lemon cream really elevates the dish.

The shortbread biscuit is made by sieving together the ground almonds, flour and icing sugar then adding the butter and beating until smooth.

Now add the eggs, the lemon zest and a pinch of salt. Wrap tightly in cling film and leave to firm up in the fridge.

Roll out the shortbread and cut into 18 circles with an 8cm cutter.

Bake in a pre-heated oven at 180°c for about 6 minutes, the biscuits should be a pale golden colour. Leave to cool on a wire rack.

For lemon cream whisk together the eggs. Boil together the lemon juice and zest with the sugar and butter and pour onto the eggs.

Cook in a heavy bottomed pan until it thickens but do not boil.

Pass it through a fine sieve and cling film to touch to prevent a skin forming.

Top and tail a large pineapple and with a large serrated knife remove the skin.

Cut it into 12 equal slices and then neaten them up with an 8cm cutter so that they are the same size as the biscuits.

Remove the cores from the slices with a smaller cutter (4cm) to allow space for the lemon cream.

Dice all the trimmings, but not the very centre core. Make a stock syrup by boiling together the water, caster sugar and vanilla. Once boiling add the diced pineapple and remove from the heat.

In a large sauté pan melt together the butter and brown sugar to make a toffee, add the pineapple slices to this, coat them in the toffee and cook for a minute on each side.

To assemble:

Dust with icing sugar, one biscuit per portion, making a criss-cross design on top with a hot needle.

Layer together the biscuits and pineapple, which should be still warm with a spoon of lemon cream in the centre of each pineapple slice, finishing with the criss-crossed biscuit.

Carefully place the diced pineapple around the outside and garnish with a little crème anglaise and some white chocolate curls.

Chef's note:

This lemon cream also makes a wonderful filling for a petits-four tartelette, try it with a very, very, thin slice of radish on top.

Chocolate & Passion Fruit Delice

Ingredients

Tiffin base

5g	milk chocolate
15g	butter
1½ tbsp	golden syrup
60g	digestive biscuits

Passion fruit gel

125g	passion fruit purée
10g	pectin, medium set
140g	sugar
25g	liquid glucose
1	pinch citric acid

Chocolate delice

170g	dark chocolate
160ml	milk
70ml	double cream
1	egg
10g	sugar

Raspberry sorbet

550ml	water
340g	sugar
575g	raspberry purée

Serves 6

This luxurious three layered dessert is sure to impress. The richness of the chocolate is delicately balanced by the passion fruit layer and the raspberry sorbet.

Tiffin base

Combine ingredients and set in a suitable deep tray approximately 15cm x 10cm.

Passion fruit gel

Boil together the passion fruit purée and 15g of the sugar.

Mix together the pectin powder with the remaining sugar, sprinkle onto the purée, whisk it in and re-boil.

Add the liquid glucose and cook to 105°c.

Finally add the citric acid, pass and pour through a strainer onto the tiffin base. Leave to set.

Chocolate delice

Make a thick créme Anglaise with the above ingredients and then pass it onto the chopped bitter chocolate, whisk to combine, cool slightly and then pour onto the passion fruit gel.

Leave to set before cutting into portions.

Raspberry Sorbet

Boil the ingredients together for 3 minutes, pass, cool and churn.

Chefs note:

When cutting this dessert dip the knife into hot water first to give a clean smooth edge.

Lemon & Mascarpone Mousse with Passion Fruit Syrup

Ingredients

Mousse

85g	sugar
50ml	lemon juice
15g	butter
½	lemon into grated zest
1	leaf of gelatine, pre-soaked in cold water
2	eggs, separated
180g	mascarpone
40ml	double cream, lightly whisked

Biscuit base

75g	ginger nut biscuits
35g	melted butter

Syrup

100ml	orange juice
35g	sugar
1	passion fruit

Biscuit garnish

35g	melted butter
35g	icing sugar, sieved
35g	flour, sieved
1	egg white

Serves 6

This is the lightest of cheesecakes, with a kick of lemon. The tuile adds a presentational flourish while the passion fruit syrup adds an extra dimension.

In a food processor, blitz the biscuits and combine with the melted butter. Layer thinly into 6 rings (7cm) on a tray and push down firmly to compact the base. Set in the fridge.

Boil together 40g of the sugar with the lemon juice, butter and lemon zest. Once boiled remove from the heat and add the gelatine making sure that it is fully dissolved.

In a food mixer whisk together 25g of the sugar with the egg yolks and then pour the lemon mix onto it.

Continue whisking until cool and then add the mascarpone to it, whisk until smooth. Fold in the cream.

Whisk together the egg whites and bit by bit the remaining sugar. Whisk to firm peaks and finally fold that into the mixture.

Fill the rings with the mousse and leave to set in the fridge for at least an hour before serving.

Cut the passion fruit in half and remove the pulp. Pass it through a sieve retaining the seeds and add the passed juice to the orange juice and sugar, then reduce until thick.

Blanche the seeds in water and then rub them in a cloth to remove any remaining pulp before adding them to the syrup. Cool and chill before using.

Biscuit

Beat the sugar with the butter, add the flour and beat again. Add the egg white and beat until free of lumps.

Cling film to touch and leave to firm up in the fridge.

With a template, bake the biscuits in triangles in a pre-heated oven at 180°c for 3-4 minutes until lightly browned.

Whilst still hot, gently shape around a circular object: be prepared to have a couple of breakages!

Serving:

Simply de-mould the mousses by warming the rings between your hands and place onto plates with the biscuit tucked in underneath. Glaze with the syrup.

White Chocolate Cheesecake with Marinated Strawberries

Ingredients

Cheesecake

3	digestive biscuits
3	ginger nut biscuits
20g	clarified butter
2	egg yolks
35g	sugar
½	leaf of gelatine soaked in cold water
10ml	double cream
100g	cream cheese, softened
85g	white chocolate, melted
100ml	lightly whipped double cream

Jelly

20g	sugar
15g	strawberry purée
30ml	sweet wine
¼	leaf of gelatine, soaked in cold water

Strawberries

100g	strawberries
10g	icing sugar
20ml	orange juice

Serves 4

In a food processor blend the biscuits into a crumb and then bind with the clarified butter. Push firmly into 7cm individual moulds to form an even base.

Bring the sugar to the boil with a drop of water and pour onto the egg yolks whisk until light and pale, Boil the 10ml double cream and dissolve the gelatine into the mix. Add it to the yolks through a tea strainer and continue whisking until cool.

Add the softened cream cheese, then the melted chocolate and finally fold in the whipped cream. Spoon on top of the biscuit bases, leaving a small gap for the jelly. Refrigerate until set.

For the jelly, bring the purée, wine and sugar to the boil. Add the soaked gelatine and then pass through a fine sieve.

Leave to cool in a fridge until almost set before topping off the cheesecakes with it.

Liquidize together 40g of the strawberries with the icing sugar and orange juice, pass through a fine sieve to remove the seeds and then quarter and add the remaining strawberries.

Leave them for at least a couple of hours to marinate.

Serving:

On the serving plates make a design with crème Anglaise.

To de-mould the cheesecakes gently warm the rings between the palms of your hands and ease them out onto the plates.

Top the cheesecakes with the marinated strawberries and place the rest of them around the cheesecake.

Chef's note:

This dessert is perfect for a summer's day.

Serve it with an ice cream or sorbet.

To add an extra kick to the marinated strawberries, add a generous drop of Grand-Marnier.

Apple & Blackberry Crumble Tart, Clotted Cream Ice Cream

Ingredients

300g	sweet pastry

Apple and blackberry mix

6	apples, peeled, cored and sliced
50g	butter
200g	blackberries
175g	soft light brown sugar
½ tsp	ground cinnamon

Crumble mix

80g	butter
80g	sugar
80g	ground almonds
100g	flour

Crème patissière

160ml	milk
35g	sugar
½	vanilla pod, split
2	yolks
15g	flour, sieved

Crème Anglaise

200ml	double cream
100ml	milk
70g	sugar
½	vanilla pod, split
4	yolks

Clotted cream ice cream

275g	milk
125g	sugar
5	yolks
225g	clotted cream
75g	double cream

Serves 8

I always dry bake the crumble first for any recipe, it always stays crunchier that way...

Start with 300g sweet pastry, rolled and blind baked in 10cm tartelette cases.

For the apple and blackberry mix, make a caramel with the sugar and then add the butter.

When foaming add the apples and the cinnamon.

Add the blackberries and heat through.

Then drain the liquid from the fruit into another pan.

Return this to the heat and cook until a syrupy consistency.

Pour back over the apple mixture and reserve.

To make the crumble, rub together and pre-bake at 180°c for 15 minutes on a baking tray, having turned and moved it around on the tray once during the cooking.

Crème patissière is made by boiling the milk and vanilla in a pan, whisking together the yolks, sugar and flour.

Once boiling add the milk to the yolk mix, whisk well and return to the pan and stir to the boil.

Once cooked remove from the heat and take out the vanilla pod, reserve until needed.
To make crème Anglaise, boil together the cream, milk, 50g of the sugar and the vanilla pod.

Beat together the yolks with the remaining sugar. Once boiling pour the milk and cream onto the yolks, mix well and return to the pan.

Cook until the sauce coats the back of a spoon.

Pass the sauce through a fine sieve and keep to one side until needed.

Clotted cream ice cream

Boil together the milk and 75g of the sugar.

Beat together the yolks with the remaining sugar.

Once boiling, pour the milk onto the yolks, mix well and return to the pan.

Cook until the sauce coats the back of a spoon.

In a bowl, mix together the clotted cream and double cream. Pass the hot liquid onto it, whisk well and leave to cool before churning in an ice cream machine.

Serving:

Fill the blind-baked cases with the apple mix and then add a spoon of crème patissière.

Top this with the crumble mixture, and place into a pre-heated oven at 180°c for 8-10 minutes.

Serve with the crème Anglaise and the clotted cream ice cream.

Chocolate & Peanut Fondant

Ingredients

Fondant

250g	dark chocolate
250g	butter
125g	sugar
50g	flour, sieved
5	whole eggs
5	yolks

Ganache

75ml	milk
60g	smooth peanut butter
100g	white chocolate

Chocolate sauce

400ml	double cream
100g	sugar
300g	dark chocolate

Peanut butter ice cream

7	egg yolks
175g	sugar
500ml	milk
500ml	double cream
1	split vanilla pod
50g	smooth peanut butter
20g	glucose

Serves 6

Chocolate and peanut combinations have been around for ages. However, this delicious but rich recipe – served with a peanut butter ice cream – gives a new twist to this terrific pairing.

Fondant

Melt the chocolate and butter in a bowl over simmering water. Whisk together the whole eggs, egg yolks and sugar and combine with the melted chocolate/butter mixture. Next, gently fold in the flour until just combined. Leave to one side.

Peanut & white chocolate ganache

For the ganache, combine the milk and peanut butter in a saucepan and bring to the boil. Remove from the heat and pour over the chopped white chocolate, whisking together until combined. Set aside in the fridge to cool.

While the ganache is cooling, grease the dariole moulds; firstly with a generous amount of butter and then cocoa powder.

Pour the chocolate fondant mixture one third of the way up the mould, then place a small drop of the ganache into the middle of the mix. Fill the remainder of the mould with the fondant mixture up to three quarters full. Set aside in the fridge until all the other elements are prepared.

Chocolate sauce

Combine the double cream and sugar and bring to the boil. Once boiling remove from the heat and pour onto the chopped dark chocolate, whisking it thoroughly to combine.

Peanut butter ice cream

Combine the milk, cream and vanilla pod in a saucepan, bring to the boil and then remove from the heat. In a large bowl, thoroughly whisk the yolks and sugar until pale and smooth.

Slowly pour the hot milk mixture over the yolks to combine and then return the mixture to the saucepan.
Place on a low to medium heat and stir constantly until it reaches 80°c.

While still warm whisk in the glucose and peanut butter and then pass through a sieve, leave to cool and then churn in an ice cream machine to reach the desired consistency.

Cooking and serving

Bake the fondants at 200°c in a preheated oven for 8-10 minutes depending on the size and shape of the mould, make sure that the mixture is set around the outside and is starting to come away from the edge. The fondant must be soft in the centre.

Turn out the fondants into a deep bowl, pour some of the chocolate sauce around and dust with icing sugar, take a ball of the ice cream and roll it into some chopped roasted peanuts and serve immediately.

Chefs note:

Do not overfill the moulds as the mixture will rise during cooking and may overflow.

Treacle & Crème Patissière Tart

Ingredients

150g	sweet pastry
80g	puff pastry

Crème patissière

150ml	milk
1	vanilla pod, split
30g	sugar
2	egg yolks
15g	flour

Treacle filling

200g	golden syrup
80g	soft white breadcrumbs

Serves 4

This is a slightly refined version of a childhood favourite of mine.

Roll 150g of sweet pastry and line 4 x 10cm tart moulds.

Pre-heat the oven to 180°c and bake them blind.

After 10-12 minutes they should have a nice golden colour and be firm to the touch.

For the crème patissière whisk together the sugar and egg yolks until light and fluffy and then fold in the flour.

Bring the milk and vanilla to the boil, pour and whisk onto the egg mixture.

Pour into a clean pan, gently bring to the boil and cook for a further minute.

Remove from the heat, remove the vanilla pod and reserve.

For the treacle filling gently warm the golden syrup and then add the soft white breadcrumbs.

Divide the crème patissière between the four tartlettes smoothing it into the bases and then top with the syrup mixture.

Roll out 80g of puff pastry and cut it into strips and make a criss-cross lattice on top.

Sprinkle the top with caster sugar and then bake in a pre-heated oven at 180°c for 15-20 minutes, until the lattice is golden.

Chef's note:

Dress onto warmed plates with a drizzle of raspberry coulis and crème anglaise.

I suggest having some spare Anglaise in a sauce jug as not only do people love it but this dessert does seem to absorb it!

Pear Soufflé with Chocolate Sauce

Ingredients

Pear purée

500g	pears
20g	soft dark brown sugar
	lemon juice

Pear crème patissière

50ml	milk
1	yolk
20g	sugar
10g	flour
100ml	pear purée

Chocolate sauce

140g	double cream
35g	sugar
100g	dark chocolate

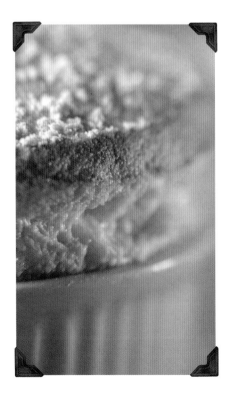

Serves 4

The skill of the soufflé..? it's all in the whites!

For the pear purée, peel and remove the cores and dice the pears. Cook them until soft with the sugar and a squeeze of lemon juice.

Once cooked, blend and pass them through a fine sieve. If necessary add a drop of water to enable it to blend.

To make the pear crème patissière (for the soufflé base) whisk together the sugar and egg yolk, fold in the flour.

Bring the milk and half the pear purée to the boil, pour and whisk onto the egg mixture.

Pour into a clean pan, gently bring to the boil and cook for a further minute. Remove from heat, and pour onto the remaining purée. The sauce is made by boiling together the double cream and sugar and pour onto the chocolate. Whisk gently to combine.

Assembling the soufflés:

Warm the crème patissière mixture. Whisk together 130g egg white (3 or 4 depending on size) with 35g of sugar. Add the sugar in at least two stages, not all at once. The whites should be stiff but not meringue! Gently fold in the crème patissière to the egg whites until well incorporated.

Spoon into pre-buttered and sugared soufflé moulds. When half full, place the remaining purée into the middle of the soufflés and then continue filling.

Clean around the edges of the moulds and also run your thumb around the edge to create a rim and bake in a pre-heated oven 200°c for approximately 8-10 minutes. Once cooked dust with icing sugar and serve immediately with the chocolate sauce.

Chef's note:

For convenience all of the elements can be prepared in advance, leaving only the whisking of the egg whites as final preparation. Butter the moulds with an upward stroke to help the soufflé rise.

Any left over chocolate sauce is great to warm through and to pour over ice cream another time.

These are... basic savoury recipes

à la Grecque

20ml	white wine vinegar
100ml	water
100ml	olive oil
3	pinch coriander seeds, then crushed
1	pinch white peppercorns
40g	tomato purée
1	lemon into juice
½ tsp	sugar
½ tsp	sea salt

Mix all together and bring to simmer for a couple of minutes.

Leave to cool before adding pre-cooked vegetables - carrots, French beans, baby onions, radishes or, my favourites, artichokes.

Blinis

15g	yeast
250ml	milk
25g	rye flour

Leave 2 hours to prove and then add:

125g	flour
2	egg yolks

Leave again for 1 hour and then add

2	egg whites, whisked to peak with a pinch of salt

Cook spoon sized blinis in a non-stick pan with a brush of oil.

As easy as that.

Bread sauce x6
(For my girls who adore it)

1	medium sized onion (150g)
50g	butter
1	bay leaf
8	cloves
500ml	milk
	salt
5	slices of bread
	double cream

Finely chop and sweat half of the onion in the butter. Stud the other half of the onion with a bay leaf and 8 cloves. Once chopped onion is cooked, but without colour, add 500ml of milk and the studded onion. Leave to cook on a very low heat to infuse. After 20 minutes add a couple of pinches of salt and 5 slices of bread, crusts off and cubed, cut the bread with a serrated knife so as not to squash it! Leave to cook again until thickened, stir the sauce with a wooden spoon or spatula or whisk if you prefer a smooth bread sauce. For extra richness add a drop of double cream or stir in a knob of unsalted butter.

Carrot ketchup

40g	sugar
40ml	water

Boil together to make a syrup and then add

300g	well cooked carrots, drained
50ml	olive oil
75ml	white wine vinegar
1	pinch dry mustard powder
	salt

Combine all of the ingredients in the blender and blend until very smooth.

Celery and sage pickle

350g	diced peeled celery
100g	finely chopped onion
175ml	white wine vinegar
175g	caster sugar
5	leaves of sage, finely chopped

Combine all of the ingredients in a saucepan, bring to the boil and cook until setting consistency.

Chilli jam

4	red peppers de-seeded and cut into a very small dice
5	red chillis cut into a very small dice
1	small piece of ginger diced small
4	cloves of garlic, crushed
5	plum tomatoes, skinned, de-seeded, diced
375g	golden caster sugar
125ml	red wine vinegar
50ml	fish sauce
	pinch of salt
1	lime

Combine all of the ingredients in a sauce pan and cook until thick. Finish with the juice of the lime.

Cider and yeast beignet batter

15g	yeast
300ml	cider, warmed
225g	flour
	salt and pepper

Whisk together all of the ingredients and leave to prove in a warm place for 1 hour before use.

Cheese scones

450g	self raising flour
110g	butter
120g	finely grated cheddar cheese
300ml	milk
	salt, a pinch of cayenne pepper and paprika

Rub together the flour and butter, add 100g of the grated cheese a pinch of salt and a touch of cayenne.

Make a well, add the milk and bring together.

Roll out to 2.5cm thick and then cut out to the required size.

Sprinkle on the remaining cheese and dust the tops with paprika.

Bake in a hot oven at 190°c until lightly golden but still a little moist inside. Timing will depend on size!

Chicken stock

700g	chicken bones or wings
2	carrots
1	onion
1	stick of celery
50g	leek
1	bay leaf
4	cloves

Rinse the carcasses in water, cover all of the ingredients in water and bring to the boil.

Reduce the heat to a simmer, skim off any fat.

Leave to cook for about 30 minutes, pass and reduce by half to give 500ml.

Curry sauce

200g   peeled and cubed apple
200g   carrots
150g   onion
10g   garlic

Sweat in oil and then add:

75g   mild curry powder
50g   tomato purée
        salt

Sweat again, cover with water or stock, cook until soft and then blend and pass. This basic sauce can then have a drop of cream or coconut milk added.

Fish stock

500g   white fish bones from flat fish, in preference sole, turbot or halibut, roes & gills removed
125g   onion
75g   leek
75g   celery
1   bay leaf
1   pinch of white peppercorns
100 ml white wine
800 ml water

Soak the fish bones in water overnight. The following day drain the bones in a colander, rinse, and sweat in olive oil in a suitable pan. Add the roughly chopped vegetables, the bay leaf and the peppercorns, sweat again and then add the white wine. Bring up to the boil and cook for a minute before adding the water. Bring up to a simmer and then reduce the heat slightly and cook for 20 minutes. Skim the surface, the stock should not boil. Pass the stock through a fine strainer, re-boil and skim the surface again of any fat, pass again and leave to cool. Refrigerate until needed.

Lamb stock

1.5kg   lamb bones
2   onions
2   carrots
1   celery stick
1   leek
½   head of garlic (optional)
125g   tomato purée
        thyme or rosemary
2   pigs trotters or a calf's foot

Roast the lamb bones until golden. Peel and roughly cut all of the vegetables, sweat them together in a large pan with the exception of the leek. Add the tomato purée to the vegetables and cook until it is going dark, add the bones, the leek and top up with water. Bring to the boil and add the herbs and trotters, reduce the heat so that the stock is just under a simmer and cook for 6 to 8 hours when the bones will be falling apart. Skim well to remove any fat throughout the cooking process. If the stock boils, fat will start to be incorporated into the stock which will make it cloudy and may give a muddy texture.

Once cooked, pass and reduce by gently boiling the stock to give 1½ litres, again skim well during this process. When cold, refrigerate and the stock will set at this point. If necessary it can then can be cubed and frozen to be taken out of the freezer and used as required.

Mint sauce x8

150ml   red wine vinegar
1   shallot, finely chopped
50g   sugar
15-20g   mint leaves, chopped

Boil together the vinegar, sugar and shallot. Leave to cool a little before adding the chopped mint.

Pear or quince chutney

750g	peeled and roughly cut pear or quince
125g	peeled and diced cooking apples
250g	peeled, de-seeded and chopped tomatoes
125g	finely chopped onion
125g	sultanas
50g	finely diced fresh ginger
2	finely grated zest of orange and their juice
300g	soft light brown sugar
300ml	white wine vinegar
½ tsp	ground cinnamon
½ tsp	ground nutmeg
½ tsp	cayenne pepper
½ tsp	salt

Incorporate all ingredients in a saucepan, bring to the boil. Simmer until of a sticky and setting consistency.

Pesto

10g	garlic cloves (peeled and chopped)
35g	basil leaves
50g	toasted pine nuts
75g	grated Parmesan
200ml	olive oil
	salt

Combine all of the ingredients in a blender and blend until reasonably smooth, adding the salt last of all.

Cranberry sauce x8

400g	cranberries
	peel and juice of orange
100 ml	red wine or port
200g	sugar

Cook until jammy consistency, remove the orange peel before serving.

Sweet potato purée

4	sweet potatoes, 1.2 kg
2	pinches of salt
2	pinches of five spice
50ml	double cream

Score the potatoes around their middles with a knife, place them onto a baking sheet which has been covered with salt and bake in a pre-heated oven 200°c for 1 hour. Once cooked, halve the potatoes and scoop out the flesh and blend in a food processor with the remaining ingredients.

Veal stock

3kg	veal bones , cut
3	onions
4	carrots
2	sticks of celery
1	leek
½	head of garlic (optional)
200g	tomato purée
2	calves feet, or four pigs trotters

Roast the veal bones until golden. Peel and roughly cut all of the vegetables, sweat them together in a large pan with the exception of the leek. Add the tomato purée to the vegetables and cook until it is going dark. Add the bones, the leek and top up with water. Bring to the boil and add the calves feet, reduce the heat so that the stock is just under a simmer and cook for 24 hours. Skim well to remove any fat throughout the cooking process. If the stock boils any fat will start to be incorporated into the stock which will make it cloudy and may give a muddy texture. Once cooked, pass and reduce by gently boiling the stock to give 2 litres, again skim well during this process. When cold, refrigerate and the stock will set at this point. If necessary, it can then can be cubed and frozen to be taken out of the freezer and used as required.

Pea and mint vinaigrette

5   sprigs of mint
250g   peas, cooked until soft with the mint stalks
         tied up with string
1   pinch of salt
2   pinch of sugar

Blend with:

100ml   white wine vinegar
25g   Dijon mustard

Gently add and blend:

300ml   olive oil
         leaves from 5 sprigs of mint

If the dressing splits in the fridge you can bring it
back together with the aid of a hand blender.

Vegetable stock

1   fennel
2   carrots
1   onion
1   leek
2   celery sticks
4   thyme sprigs
1   bay leaf
4   cloves
1.2l   water

Prepare and cut the vegetables, cover with the water
and add the remaining ingredients.

Bring to the boil.

Simmer for 45 minutes before passing through a fine
sieve.

Yorkshire pudding batter x12

250g   flour
4   whole eggs
400ml   milk
50ml   water
         salt and pepper

Whisk everything together in a bowl until smooth.
Pass through a sieve and refrigerate overnight for best
results.

Halve the recipe for a family toad in the hole!

Tomato ketchup

50g   chopped shallot
1   clove of garlic, crushed
6   ripe tomatoes, 400g, quartered
2tsp   tomato purée
50g   soft dark brown sugar
35ml   red wine vinegar
3   pinches of salt

In a suitable pan cook all of the ingredients together.
Pass through a fine sieve and thicken by reduction
or with a touch of corn flour mixed with a touch of
water.

Tapenade

200g   black olives, stones removed
10g   cloves of garlic, crushed
10g   salted anchovy fillets
10g   capers
100ml   olive oil

Place all in a blender and blend until a smooth paste.

These are... basic sweet recipes

Brandy snaps

85g	butter
170g	caster sugar
85g	golden syrup

Beat together and then add

85g	sieved flour

Beat until smooth, roll into balls and bake on a silicone mat or baking parchment in the oven at 180°c for about 5-6 minutes until golden, leave to cool a little before rolling or shaping. Always reminds me of Saturday mornings with my mum.

Caramel sauce

100g	sugar
75g	soft butter

Cook the above to a caramel and then carefully add

250ml	double cream

Re-boil and pass through a sieve before serving hot or cold.

Honeycomb

50g	caster sugar
15g	clear honey
50g	glucose
5g	bicarbonate of soda

Boil together the sugar, honey and glucose until dark golden, add the bicarbonate of soda and whisk. Pour onto a baking sheet or parchment, be ready for it to double in size! Leave to go cold before using.

Chocolate paint

Make a syrup from

35g	glucose
130ml	water
80g	sugar

Sieve together

120g	dark chocolate
40g	cocoa powder

Pour the syrup onto the above, pass through a sieve and leave to go cold before using.

Cigarette biscuits

100g	egg whites (3)
100g	icing sugar
100g	melted butter
100g	flour

Whisk the egg whites and gradually add the icing sugar, beat until it forms stiff peaks, add the melted butter and finally fold in the sieved flour. Spread thinly in circles on a baking mat and cook at 190°c for 5 minutes. Cool a little and then roll them up.

Lemon curd

2	whole eggs
3	egg yolks
55g	caster sugar
90ml	lemon juice
100g	butter

Combine the yolks and whole eggs, sugar and lemon in a bowl. Whisk then mix over a bain-marie until thick.

Crème Anglaise

200ml   double cream
100ml   milk
70g   sugar
½   vanilla pod, split
4   yolks

Boil together the cream, milk, 50g of the sugar and the vanilla pod.

Beat together the yolks with the remaining sugar.

Once boiling pour the milk and cream onto the yolks, mix well and return to the pan, cook until the sauce coats the back of a spoon.

Pass the sauce through a fine sieve and refrigerate with cling film to touch, until needed.

Crème pâtissière

160ml   milk
35g   sugar
½   vanilla pod, split
2   yolks
15g   flour, sieved

Boil the milk and vanilla in a pan.

Whisk together the yolks, sugar and flour.

Once boiling add the milk to the yolk, mix, whisk well and return to the pan and stir to the boil.

When cooked, remove from the heat and take out the vanilla pod. Reserve until needed with cling film to touch.

Lime syrup

2   limes prepared into juice and finely grated
        zest
120ml   water

Pour juice into a pan and add zest.

Top up with water to 120ml, cook to 105°c . Leave to go cold before use.

Croquant biscuit

400g   sieved icing sugar
130g   flour
2 pinch   mixed spice
2 pinch   five spice
1 pinch   cinnamon
160ml   milk
120g   melted butter

Sieve the dry ingredients and add the wet and beat with a food mixer. Spread thinly onto a baking mat and bake at 180°c until golden. Cool slightly before removing.

Mulled wine (for Sara H!)

1.5l   red wine
1.5l   orange juice
2   oranges (peel for wine, slices for garnish)
1   star anise
24   juniper berries
1   cinnamon stick
12   cloves
1   bay leaf
300g   demerara sugar

Boil, cover and leave to infuse until cold. Pass through a strainer into bottles. Serve hot when needed.

Sponge fingers

3   eggs
95g   caster sugar
90g   flour
15g   icing sugar, for dusting

Separate the eggs, beat the yolks with two thirds of the sugar with a food mixer until light in colour.

Whisk the whites, slowly adding the rest of the sugar until firm to make a meringue.

Fold a third of this into the yolks and then fold in the remainder.

Sieve the flour and lastly fold this into mix.

Pipe as required leaving a gap of 4cm between rows.

Dust with icing sugar and bake for 8-10 minutes at 200°c.

Shortcrust pastry

250g   flour
150g   butter
1 tsp   salt
1   pinch of sugar
1   egg

Crumb the flour and butter.

Add the salt, sugar and egg and then bind with 1 tablespoon of milk.

Form into a rectangular shape, cling film and refrigerate to rest for at least 30 minutes.

The Masons Arms Fudge

Melt together over a bain-marie 375g of white chocolate and 60g of butter

750g   sugar
250g   glucose
350ml   double cream

Cook the sugar, glucose and cream to 121°c with the aid of a sugar thermometer.

Remove from the heat and add the chocolate and butter.

Pour into a tray lined with baking parchment and leave to set before cutting into cubes.

Raspberry coulis

250g   raspberries
50g   sugar
1   lemon into juice

Boil together the raspberries, sugar and lemon juice until liquid, leave to cool a little.

Place into a blender.

Blend until smooth, pass through a sieve to remove seeds.

Refrigerate until needed.

If the raspberries are a little sour or the coulis is sharp when complete, sieve a little icing sugar into it to sweeten.

Sweet pastry

225g	flour
140g	butter
55g	caster sugar
1	egg

Cream together the butter and sugar before rubbing in the flour to crumb and bind with the egg.

Shape into a rectangle, cling film and refrigerate to rest for at least 30 minutes.

Brandy sauce

35g	butter
35g	flour
500ml	milk
125g	sugar
75ml	double cream
75ml	brandy

Melt the butter in a heavy bottomed pan, add the flour and make into a roux.

Add the milk bit by bit stirring with a spatula and bringing it back to the boil each time.

Finally add the sugar, cream and brandy.

Bring back to the boil.

Pass through a fine sieve, cling film to touch to prevent a skin forming and reserve until needed.

Chef's note:

If you feel that your Christmas needs it add up to double the brandy!!!

Christmas pudding

400g	raisins
200g	sultanas
200g	currants
130g	nibbed almonds
250g	suet
1	orange, zest and juice
1	lemon, zest and juice
1	apple, peeled and grated
1	carrot, peeled and grated
150g	fresh white breadcrumbs
160g	flour
275g	demerara sugar
4	eggs
½ tsp	salt
½ tsp	cinnamon
2 tsp	mixed spice
80g	mixed peel
80g	glacé cherries
65ml	brandy
180ml	Guinness

This will make enough for 2 bowls, 750ml, with 8 portions in each. Mix together the dry ingredients and combine them with the wet ingredients, leave in the fridge for 48 hours to mature.

Put into pudding bowls and cover with greaseproof paper, cover the top of the bowl with tin foil.

Place into a deep dish with a cloth at the bottom and filled with water at least to half way up the bowls.

Cook at 140°c for 8 hours.

At the time of serving reheat thoroughly.

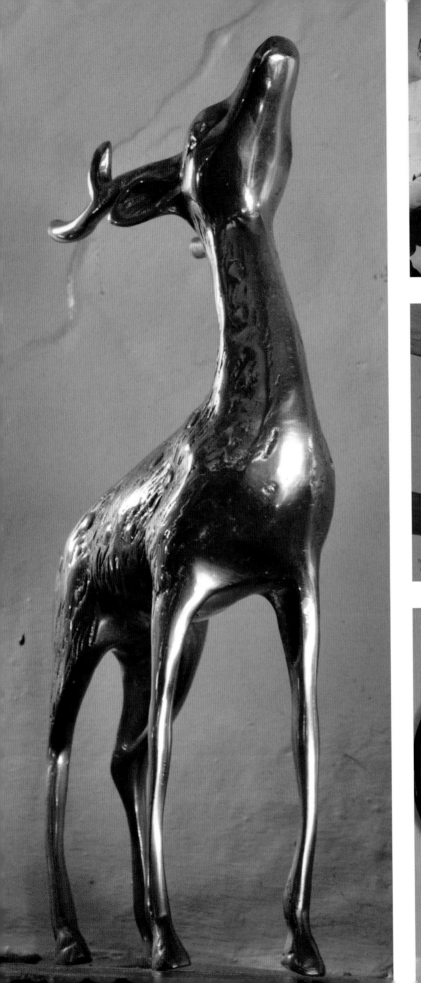

Index

Mousse; Lemon & Mascarpone Mousse with Passion Fruit Syrup, **176**

Mushroom; Puff Pastry of Mushroom Duxelles with St Enodoc Asparagus, Poached Egg & Hollandaise Sauce, **54**

Mussels; Pappardelle with Mussels and Roquefort, **70**

O

Orange; Breast of Duck with Orange Sauce & Pommes Berny, **96**

P

Panna Cotta, Cream Cheese Panna Cotta with Caramelised Pineapple, **164**

Pappardelle; Pappardelle with Mussels and Roquefort, **70**

Partridge; Roasted Partridge with Stuffed Cabbage & Tarragon Jus, **136**

Passion Fruit; Chocolate & Passion Fruit Delice, **174**

Pasta; **30**

Pea; Croquette of Ham Hock with Pea Purée, Mint Butter Sauce, **60**

Peanut; Chocolate & Peanut Fondant, with peanut butter ice cream **184**

Pear; Loin of Venison with Poached Pear & Blue Cheese Gratin, **144**

Pear Soufflé with Chocolate Sauce, **188**

Seared Scallops served with Pear & Vanilla, **52**

Pineapple; Cream Cheese Panna Cotta with Caramelised Pineapple, **164**

Pineapple, Shortbread and Lemon Cream, **172**

Pork; Pork Fillet with Potato, Prosciutto & Parmesan Gratin, **102**

Pork Belly with Braised Red Cabbage & Apple Compôte, **104**

Potato; Potato Pancakes with Cèpe Mushrooms, **68**

Potato Fondant, **120**

Poussin; Poussin with Peppers, Potato Rösti & Tarragon Jus, **92**

Prosciutto Ham; Monkfish Loin wrapped in

Prosciutto Ham, Potato Purée, Orange & Balsamic Sauce, **76**

Prosciutto; Pork Fillet with Potato, Prosciutto & Parmesan Gratin, 102

Pheasant; Breast of Pheasant with Choucroute & Sausage, **138**

Q

Quail; Breasts of Quail with Grapes, Walnuts & Sauternes Jus, **56**

R

Rabbit; Stuffed Saddle of Rabbit, Parsley Risotto & Spring Vegetables, **86**

Red Cabbage; Pork Belly with Braised Red Cabbage & Apple Compôte, **104**

Red Mullet; Fillets of Red Mullet with Bouillon, **78**

Red Wine; Braised Beef Cheek in Red Wine, **124**

Beef Wellington, Potato Gratin & Red Wine Jus, **130**

Rhubarb; Duck Liver Parfait, Rhubarb Chutney, **48**

Rhubarb & Sweet Wine Trifle, **158**

Risotto; Smoked Haddock Risotto with Parmesan & a Poached Egg, Grain Mustard Sauce, **62**

Risotto; Stuffed Saddle of Rabbit, Parsley Risotto & Spring Vegetables, **86**

S

Salad; Salad of Crab with Orange & Star Anise, **40**

Soy, Mirin & Yuzu Marinated Salmon, Salad of White Radish, Apple & Cucumber, **44**

Smoked Chicken with Thai Style Salad, **34**

Salmon; Black Treacle-Cured Salmon, **36**

Hot smoked salmon with crab and aïoli, **72**

Soy, Mirin & Yuzu Marinated Salmon, Salad of White Radish, Apple & Cucumber, **44**

Scallops; Smoked Scallops with Wasabi, Noodles & Vermouth Sauce, **58**

Sea Bass; Fillet of Sea Bass with Jerusalem Artichoke Purée, Roasted Garlic, Butter Beans, Flageolets & Red Wine Jus, **82**

Shallots; Beef Fillet served with Roasted Shallots & Sauté Potatoes and a Green Peppercorn Sauce, **128**

Shellfish; Shellfish Bisque with Sole Raviolo, **30**

Sole; Shellfish Bisque with Sole Raviolo, **30**

Sorrel; Turbot Cooked on the Bone with Sorrel Sauce, **80**

Suet Pudding; Lamb Confit Suet Pudding, **106**

Sweetbreads; Loin of lamb with Sweetbreads, Aubergine Purée & Boulangère Potatoes, **108** Pan Roasted Veal Sweetbreads served with Sauce Diable, **118**

T

Tarragon; Poussin with Peppers, Potato Rösti & Tarragon Jus, **92**

Tempura batter, **78**

Toffee; Toffee & Banana Mille-Feuille, **168**

Tomato; Roasted Tomato & Garlic Soup with Croûtons, **28**

Treacle; Treacle & Crème Patissière Tart, **186**

Trifle; Rhubarb & Sweet Wine Trifle, **158**

Truffle; Breast of Corn-Fed Chicken, Truffled Sausage, Potato Purée with Leeks, Thyme Jus, **90**

Tuna; Seared Peppered Tuna with Oriental Salad, **42**

Turbot; Turbot Cooked on the Bone with Sorrel Sauce, **80**

V

Veal; Pan Roasted Veal Sweetbreads served with Sauce Diable, **118**

Veal Chop served with Sage & Parmesan Crust, **120**

Venison; Loin of Venison with Poached Pear & Blue Cheese Gratin, **144**

W

Wasabi; Smoked Scallops with Wasabi, Noodles & Vermouth Sauce, **58**

White Chocolate; White Chocolate Cheesecake with Marinated Strawberries, **178**

Wild Duck; Wild Duck with Fig & Cranberries, **140**

Woodcock; Traditional Roasted Woodcock served on a Croûton, **152**

Wood Pigeon; Breasts of Wood Pigeon with Curried Brussels Sprout Purée & Stuffing, **134**

Y

Yoghurt; Chicken in a Brick with Spice & Yoghurt, **88**

The Masons Arms

Credits and Thank Yous

First published in Great Britain in 2017 by A Way With Media Ltd, Shrewsbury, SY3 7LN

Copyright © Mark Dodson 2017

The right of Mark Dodson to be identified as the author of this work has been asserted by him in accordance with the Copyright, Designs and Patents Act 1988

A CIP catalogue record for this book is available from the British Library.

ISBN:
9781910469118

Credits:

Writer and Food Styling
Mark Dodson

Additional Food Styling
Jess Delahaye

Editorial Assistants
Sarah Dodson
Kate Harvey

Editorial Design and Production
Paul Naylor

Publisher, Photographer, Editor
Andy Richardson

My huge thanks to Sarah for putting up with me and my book for the last 12 months, you are my star.

To Jess Delahaye for helping to lovingly create these dishes for photographing.

To Kate Harvey for reading through too many recipes too many times,
asserting grammatical control and for tireless Kateproofing.

To Michel Roux who has written so many books - I take my hat off to you!

To Paul Naylor for the brilliant design and for bringing my book to life.

Last but not least to Andy Richardson, without whom this book would never have happened.
Who would have thought that a passing comment and a mutual love of music would lead to This Is Mine?